Climbing: From Single Pitch to Multipitch

Ron Funderburke

FALCONGUIDES

GUILFORD, CONNECTICUT

FALCONGUIDES®

An imprint of The Rowman & Littlefield Publishing Group, Inc.
4501 Forbes Blvd., Ste. 200
Lanham, MD 20706
www.rowman.com
Falcon and FalconGuides are registered trademarks and Make
Adventure Your Story is a trademark of The Rowman & Littlefield
Publishing Group, Inc.

Distributed by NATIONAL BOOK NETWORK

British Library Cataloguing in Publication Information available

Library of Congress Cataloging-in-Publication Data available

ISBN 978-1-4930-2766-8 (paperback)
ISBN 978-1-4930-2767-5 (e-book)

∞™ The paper used in this publication meets the minimum
requirements of American National Standard for Information
Sciences—Permanence of Paper for Printed Library Materials,
ANSI/NISO Z39.48-1992.

Printed in the United States of America

Contents

Introduction

In Yosemite Valley, California, many climbers experience their first rock climbs on the pristine (if heavily polished) granite of the Swan Slabs, 40- to 100-foot climbs nestled beneath the soaring majesty of the walls that prop up the cascading Yosemite Falls. In many cases the climber that tops out her first rock climb on the Swan Slab arches her eyes up and up to take in the grandeur that looms far beyond her modest summit. She is captivated. She is curious, and she intuits that rock climbing is far bigger than the 60-foot slab she has just accomplished.

I'm willing to stipulate that the imagination of every climber can be prodded in this way. Beyond the anchors of every toprope, beyond the mussy hooks of any sport climb, beyond the last awkward jam of

Toproping is fun, but eventually some climbers will wonder how to climb past their chains.

The Swan Slabs are amazing, but these walls inspire a grander vision.

the most rugged trad climb, a world awaits. For the climber in Yosemite, the presence of that world is conspicuous and it is inescapable, but the climber in Wisconsin might have to telescope far beyond the horizon to sense what she might be missing. The climber in the gyms of Houston, Texas, might have to flip through the pages of a magazine or troll the Instagram feed of his heroes to see the giant cliffs casting shadows on his local haunts. Regardless of a climber's proximity to multipitch climbing, regardless of his affection for boulders or crags or climbing gyms, the imagination of any climber can be steered from a single pitch of excitement to multiple enduring pitches of elation.

When that curiosity strikes, the contents of this book are hopefully available. Multipitch climbing is not the inevitable outcome of single-pitch climbing. Many climbers will stand atop the Swan Slabs and yearn for the smaller boulders in the shade of the oak trees. Many climbers will avert the long hikes, the backpacks, the heavy racks, and the panic attacks, opting for what's manageable, compact, and comfortable. But some wanderlusting, yearning souls will want to know how to climb past the chains. For them, I offer this little tome.

When combined with great instruction, great mentorship, great training, and great preparation, the rewards of multipitch climbing are replete with splendor, with adventure, and with mystery.

CHAPTER 1

Defining Multipitch

In a way this is the book that should allow both the readers and the writer to do away with all the fencing that we put around the other books in this series. Multipitch climbing, in theory, should encompass all the disciplines and an appreciation of all the skills that are covered in other texts in this series. It will involve basic toproping skills like anchoring and equipment use, but the typical counterweight arrangement involved in belaying a toprope setup will evolve into various manifestations of direct belaying. Much like any sport climb, this text will involve lead climbing and belaying lead climbing, but leading from a suspended stance or belaying a leader from that stance is substantially different than sport climbing. The leader has the ability to create lead fall forces that are impressively large, and the belayer is then forced to contend with and defend herself from those forces.

Much like traditional climbing, all multipitch climbs can be characterized as an adventurous (and therefore risky) pursuit. But the skills needed to access multipitch climbs unveil risks that dramatically increase in severity. The difference between the risk and commitment involved in any two single-pitch trad climbs can never be as vast or as dangerous as the difference between a two-pitch climb and a twenty-pitch climb. Yet, they are both considered multipitch climbs.

Furthermore, many texts written on the subject of multipitch climbing sustain the myth that there is a distinction between multipitch sport and multipitch trad. In continuation of the distinctions made in our sport-climbing text and our trad-climbing text, this text will dispel that distinction entirely. Because all multipitch climbs create an arrangement where a belayer is suspended in 5th-Class terrain, they all create situations where problems cannot be solved by a quick lower to the ground and an even quicker evacuation. So they all flirt with the unknown in a way that single-pitch climbs do not. Therefore, the presence of permanent anchors and protection bolts seems particularly irrelevant. Retreat from these anchors is only slightly less time-consuming than a cliff without bolts, though abandoning removable anchors is substantially more costly.

The consequences of mishap in a multipitch environment are also dramatically compounded by the size and relative expertise of the climbing team. In single pitch an experienced climber might serve as mentor to an inexperienced climber, and the cost of the learning curve might simply be overall efficiency. By contrast, an inexperienced participant in multipitch climb is usually unequipped to assist his more experienced partner. If she is injured (which is most likely to happen to a lead climber regardless of experience), she cannot rely on her partner to execute a complex improvised rescue. Similarly, large multipitch teams (more than two climbers) necessitate vastly more intricate rope craft, and the time required to complete a large objective multiplies rapidly. Plus, large teams congest tiny ledges and anchors.

In all these distinctions we'll also have to take some time to explain what multipitch rock climbing is not. We'll explore the difference between multipitch free climbing and big-wall climbing, via implements of aid or otherwise. We'll have to explore the difference between alpine rock climbing and regular rock climbing. We'll have to explore the difference between rock climbing and scrambling, and we'll have to distinguish multipitch rock from other climbing mediums like ice and snow.

Teams of three require complicated rope work, and they crowd tiny ledges. Teams of three require more-advanced skills.

Snow is actually a hazardous obstacle if it's not managed appropriately. Snow is hopefully not a part of multipitch rock climbing.

Accordingly, we'll define multipitch rock climbing within the following parameters:

- A free climb.
- A climb that involves a 5th-Class objective.
- 2nd-, 3rd-, and 4th-Class difficulties may be required to access or egress the 5th-Class objective, but the 5th-Class climbing should be the objective.

- The climb requires one or more intermediate belays to ascend and/or descend.
- The climbing team consists of two people.
- Both members of the climbing team have achieved a minimum competency through ground school, guidance, or instruction.

Mountaineers want to climb mountains; rock climbers want to climb rocks. Mountaineering requires different skills than rock climbing.

Historic or Famous Climb	Is This Climb an MP Rock Climb?	Why or Why Not?
Cables Route on Longs Peak, CO	No	Most of the time, there is a short section of snow climbing needed to access the Cables Route. It begins at over 13,000 ft., so altitude sickness is a possibility. As a result, the Cables Route is more of an alpine climb.
The Nose of Looking Glass Rock, NC, with three people	Probably not	While the Nose would be a great objective for a party of 2, with 3 people the ledges become cramped, the rope work becomes complex, and the party tends to clog the route for an extraordinary amount of time. Only advanced parties navigate this route as a party of 3 effectively.
Mom takes her 13-year-old son up the Kor-Ingalls route on the Castleton Tower	Probably not	If this teenager cannot effectively rescue his mother from the climb, the team is not MP rock climbing. Mom is effectively guiding her son, and guiding is different than rock climbing.
Torment Peak, North Cascades National Park, WA	No	Never mind the glaciers and perennial snow deposition, Torment Peak is not climbed as a 5th-Class objective. It's climbed for its elusive summit. 5th-Class climbing is not the motivation for climbing; it's just one of many obstacles from the summit.

Historic or Famous Climb	Is This Climb an MP Rock Climb?	Why or Why Not?
The Nose of El Capitan, Yosemite Valley, CA	No	It is very difficult to climb the Nose without a bivouac somewhere along the route, either on the way up or the way down. Climbing it usually involves hauling bivouac equipment for all but the most advanced teams.
High Exposure, Shawangunks, NY	Yes	A minimally skilled team can climb High Exposure in 2 or 3 pitches and descend 2 adjacent rappels.
Ed's Crack, Vedauwoo, WY	Yes	A minimally skilled team can ascend Ed's Crack in 2 or 3 pitches and scramble down from the top of the feature.
Playing Hooky, Clear Creek Canyon, CO	Yes	Even though bolts protect the entire climb, the exposed position high on the climb cannot be quickly evacuated. It's a multipitch adventure.
Serenity Crack into Sons of Yesterday, Yosemite Valley, CA	Yes	Two climbers that can both lead 5.10 efficiently can climb up Serenity/Sons and descend during the daylight hours of any fall or spring day.

- Frozen precipitation (snow or ice) is either completely avoided or altogether absent from any portion of the objective.

- Altitude sickness is highly unlikely on the climb.

- Bivouac is not required during a timely ascent and descent.

Commitment

Multipitch terrain can include as many pitches as a climbing team can climb in a day, or it can include two or three portions of a rope length. It can be right beside the road, or it can require hours of hiking to access. To quantify this aspect of multipitch climbing, commitment grades are typically assigned. It's important to understand what a commitment grade indicates. It's not an indication of the commitment required by the fastest team; fast teams are exposed to 5th-Class terrain for less time. Nor is it an indication of the commitment required by the slowest team; slow teams are exposed to 5th-Class terrain for more time.

Instead, commitment grades integrate a mean stipulation about the capabilities of the average climbing team. The average climbing team may struggle to climb the most difficult pitches on a multipitch climb. The leader may take falls, or she might require multiple attempts to decipher a crux sequence. Similarly, her equally skilled partner might also struggle to second those same moves. On approach, the average party hikes at a moderate pace, and the average party may need a little extra time to find the exact route up to a climb and down from it. These predictable uses of time and these predictable inefficiencies are hallmarks of almost all climbing parties on routes that challenge them, unfamiliar approaches and descents, and the careful but efficient execution of transitions from hiking to climbing, from one pitch to the next, from climbing to rappelling, and from rappelling to hiking. Average climbing teams do all these things.

It's important to assume the perspective of an average party when considering commitment grades. Put the level of commitment in that context, and grades are rarely disputed. The ability of an advanced party to make short work of an easy climb should not undermine or dispute the value of a commitment grade. Commitment grades are supposed to presume a level of technical proficiency, and it cannot be understated: Technical deficiency can make any climb more committing than it might typically be for an average party.

Grade I. A single-pitch climb that can be completed in a short climbing session.

Grade II. A single-pitch climb with a complex approach and descent or a short multipitch climb that requires less than half a business day to complete. A climbing team should be able to leave the car, complete the climb, and return to the car in less than 4 hours.

Grade III. A multipitch climb that requires a business day to complete. A climbing team should be able to leave the car, complete the climb, and return to the car in less than 8 hours.

Grade IV. A multipitch climb that requires all of the daylight hours to complete. Some days in some parts of the world at some times of year are much longer. It might be helpful to imagine these climbs in terms of the longest days of the year. It would take a climbing team less than 12 hours to leave the car, complete the climb, and return to the car.

Grade V and above require more than a day to complete. Bivouacs are typically involved in Grade V climbing and therefore they rarely qualify as multipitch rock climbing for the average party.

Commitment Grade	Description	Classic Example
Grade I	Single pitch. A short climbing session.	The Incredible Handcrack, Indian Creek, UT
Grade II	A half-day climb. Less than 4 hours to complete.	Bastille Crack, Eldorado Canyon, CO
Grade III	A business-day climb. Less than 8 hours to complete.	Tits and Beer, Looking Glass Rock, NC
Grade IV	An all-day climb. Less than 12 hours to complete.	Epinephrine, Red Rock, NV
Grade V and up	Multiday climbs. Require bivouac.	Big-wall and alpine rock climbs

Length

The length of a climb also clearly distinguishes it as a multipitch climb, but that might not be as plain and matter-of-fact as it seems. Climbers tend to see and define terrain in terms of the coincidence of a rope's length and the cliffs that are segmented by portions of that rope. If a climber takes 60m as something other than the arbitrary length to which a climbing rope has been manufactured and trimmed, it is not difficult to imagine a 150-foot cliff as a long single pitch, and nothing but a single pitch. But a 30-foot rope, the ability to anchor along any line of weakness, and the ability to manage a belay at any stance, turns the same 150-foot cliff into a five-pitch climb.

We'll recommend exercises like that for training and practice, but for the moment it serves to clarify how the length of a climb is a criterion for multipitch. Though there are many noteworthy exceptions, most multipitch rock climbs are longer than 150 feet.

Climbing Team

The composition and net competence of a climbing team is an inextricable part of multipitch rock climbing. Both members of a party have to have comparable technical proficiency, otherwise a true partnership cannot occur. Technical competence is something we will explore at length in this book, but both members of a climbing team should be proficient with preparation and research; equipment selection, care, and maintenance; lead belaying and lead climbing; managing a rope stance on ledges, semi-ledges, and hanging stances; multistage rappelling; small-teams rescue; and evacuation procedures.

If both members are not equally skilled, there will come a time in the course of a climb when the less proficient climber will be forced to rely on the expertise and skill of the more proficient climber. In that moment the more proficient climber is exposed to the incompetence of his partner, and he might not be physically, mentally, or technically prepared for that responsibility if an accident were to occur.

These unequal partnerships are not uncommon. Guided parties are composed of these unequal pairings most of the time. But a guide usually has expertise and training in guiding, and so the guide is physically, mentally, and technically prepared to deal with an incident. When average recreational lead climbers take on the responsibilities of a guide without being prepared to do so, we are going to call out that behavior as irresponsible, selfish, and foolhardy. The second that would follow that leader up those climbs bears responsibility for this temerity as well. There are better ways to learn to climb, and we should all have enough common sense not to follow every hand that beckons.

Free Climbing

The distinguishing sensation of the modern climbing era is free climbing. The climbing team that can move continuously over stone, solving puzzles of movement and athleticism, experiences something entirely unlike the siege work that pioneering climbers endured as they inched their way up multipitch climbs. An epoch ago climbing teams would resort to points of aid or assistance to climb impassable sections. Today, we climb those sections with our climbing shoes, our fingertips, and our wits.

Since modern climbing is defined by free climbing, multipitch rock climbing is defined by it as well. Today's multipitch climbing teams can select a free climb that offers appropriate challenge and the Yosemite Decimal System provides the metric for finding a free climb that best suits the climbing team. But unlike single-pitch sport and trad climbs, the difficulty of a multipitch climb is compounded by its

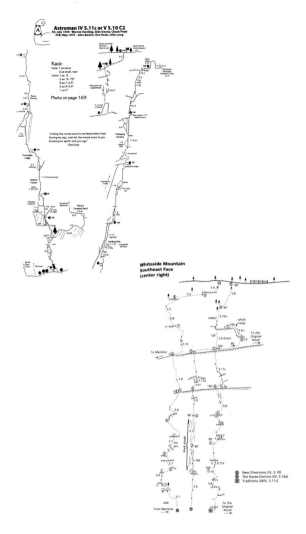

Astroman IV 5.11c or V 5.10 C2
FA: July 1959 - Warren Harding, Glen Denny, Chuck Pratt
FFA: May 1975 - John Bachar, Ron Kauk, John Long

Rack:
Nuts: 1 ea micro
2 ea small, med
Cams: 1 ea .3
2 ea .5-.75"
3 ea 1-2.5"
2 ea 3-3.5"
1 ea 4"

Photo on page 163

"Letting the moves come to me feels better than
forcing my way. Just let the moves come to you.
Extend your spirit, not your ego"
-Ron Kauk

**Whiteside Mountain
Southeast Face
(center right)**

To Mainline

To The
Original
Route

New Diversions (IV, 5.10)
The Route Doctors (IV, 5.12a)
Traditions (III/IV, 5.11c)

From Mainline

To The
Original
Route

*Even though both of these climbs are long and
committing, and they are both graded 5.11, the
stamina needed to complete a climb like the
Rostrum vastly outweighs the stamina needed to
climb the Original Route on Whiteside.*

length and the commitment required to complete the entire climb. Free-climbing teams that take too many falls on every pitch might not be able to climb an entire climb in a reasonable amount of time. As a result, climbing teams should balance their free-climbing ability and overall stamina with the cumulative difficulties of a multipitch climb.

Motivation

The team's motivation in multipitch rock climbing is also a unique distinguishing factor. Typically, the combined aesthetic quality of the climbing, the free-climbing challenges, the access to remote places, and the challenge of the entire endeavor uniquely motivate the climbing team. Aesthetics alone can be matched with less risky and less committing endeavors. Free-climbing challenges alone can be found on

It's a good thing these climbers brought their rain coats—they won't be getting out of this weather anytime soon.

single-pitch climbs. Remote places abound throughout the earth, and one doesn't need to multipitch climb to find solitude. The multipitch climbing team is usually motivated by a combination of these factors.

Exposure

Lastly, multipitch climbs expose the climbing team to an array of environmental hazards in a unique way. With a belay attached to an anchor, with a leader or second tethered to the belayer by the climbing rope, the team cannot quickly evacuate from extreme temperatures, lightning, or other inclement weather. With the team effectively chained to the cliff and to one another, the fate of one climber often enlists the fate of the other. It is difficult to escape rockfall events or falling debris. Lastly, much like distance swimmers, multipitch climbers can ascend to points where retreat is just as treacherous as continuation. Accidents can strand injured team members in inaccessible portions of a long climb. The team might not be far from advanced medical care, but they might as well be on the moon since the capabilities of rescue services vary wildly from one place to the next. In total the multipitch climbing team is exposed to environmental hazards in ways that should not be underestimated and in ways that are unique to the discipline.

Planning and Preparation

Since multipitch rock climbing is defined as an activity that requires substantial commitment, exposes the climbing team to environmental hazards in a way that cannot be easily escaped, and could require a long time to complete, planning and preparation become imperative exercises. Unlike a casual crag outing or a trip to the climbing gym, a multipitch rock climb should be thoughtfully undertaken. A team should do their homework and research, make a solid plan, and carefully prepare the climb team and its equipment for the ascent.

This chapter is divided into three main phases. In the first a climbing team is just dreaming, just thumbing through guidebooks and magazines, listening to stories, browsing the internet. This is the stuff that dreams are made of, but not every dream is practical or realistic. We'll need some tools for separating dreams from goals; we'll need to learn how to pick a climb and find a partner for that climb. In the second phase, once a climb is picked, we'll go through all the research, planning, and preparations that should happen before the climbing team even leaves the house. Finally, we'll discuss assembling equipment and an entire climbing kit, based on a time plan and topo analysis.

Phase One: Choosing a Climb

Choosing a climb should not be as random as tossing darts at a road map, nor should it be as robotic and indiscriminate as an alphabetical checklist. It should start from a place that is not rational nor mathematical. The first impetus to climb a climb should come from an ephemeral and emotional place. It should come from the psyche, the intrinsic motivation that captivates all climbers. Maybe a photo creates that spark, maybe a video or a narrative shared on social media, maybe a historic or iconic climb, maybe the sight of the climb itself, maybe the recommendation of an admired or respected climber. Either way, the psyche initiates the research, the study, and the planning. Without it, planning and preparation seem tedious, and the climb itself will seem empty and fatuous if the motivation to climb it does not come from somewhere deep inside.

Researching a Climb

Once you've selected a climb, it's time to congratulate the irrational emotional part of your subconscious for the fire that it lights, but once that fire is lit, your rational discerning mind must prevail. It must stifle that fire, save it for another day, or extinguish it altogether, by answering some key questions:

AM I CAPABLE OF CLIMBING THIS CLIMB?

- Have I climbed difficulties like this before? How did that go?
- Have I climbed something this committing before? How did that go?

- Have I climbed on this rock type, this movement style, this protection style before? How did that go?

WITH WHOM SHOULD I CLIMB IT?

- When I ask my partner the questions above, what are his/her answers?
- Is my partner capable? Does my partner have enough/appropriate equipment? Does my partner agree with my time plan?
- Which partner would be ideal? Which partner would be a nightmare?

WHEN SHOULD I CLIMB IT?

- In what season, at what time of year should I climb this climb? When would it be ideal? When would it be a nightmare?
- At what time of day should I climb this climb?
- How will timing affect the environmental hazards?
- How will timing affect the number of other parties I am likely to encounter?

EQUIPMENT CAPABILITIES:

- Do I have enough/appropriate equipment to complete this climb?
- Is my rack sufficient?
- Do I have enough rope?
- Do I have the right apparel and footwear?

The answer to each of these questions should be resounding and affirmative. If not, if the team is vacillating or unsure of even one of these points, then the rational mind must prevail. The team should pick another objective or gain more experience and expertise through training, practice, and single-pitch climbing.

Climbing Capabilities

Candor and self-awareness are vital when analyzing and assessing your own climbing abilities, and that is especially true of free-climbing difficulties. When you want to do something, it's easy to see what you want to see, to believe what you want to believe about your own abilities. Such illusions are remarkably resilient, and you may be well into your ill-considered climbing before the extent of your self-deception is revealed. We say things to ourselves like, "I climb 5.10 in the gym all the time. This climb is rated 5.10, so it should not be a problem." In truth the free-climbing grade is only one discreet factor that we use to characterize a rock climb. Our capabilities are, of course, relative to all the other factors as well: rock type, commitment, protection difficulty, and movement style.

Rock type. Multipitch climbs are available on every rock type. From granite to sandstone, limestone to volcanic, and every metamorphic shape and variety of all those, each rock type requires a slightly different expertise to climb. In general, a climber should avoid the coincidence of novelty and peak difficulty. If you've never climbed a given rock type before, consider some single-pitch climbing or bouldering on that same rock type before getting fully invested in a multipitch climb.

Commitment. Commitment is a similar proposition. If you are considering doing a Grade IV, it would be wise to have climbed a handful of Grade IIIs, and that applies all the way down the scale. Do single pitch before multipitch, climb Grade IIs before Grade IIIs, Grade IIIs before IVs, and IVs before doing climbs that are so long they take multiple days to complete. If you do a Grade IV and you have a bad experience, scale back to Grade III for a while.

Roofs are strenuous. It's important to practice features like this before they become insurmountable obstacles.

Movement. Movement style is also a notorious herring. Don't trick yourself into thinking that unfamiliar movement styles can't be that much different than familiar movement styles. You'll be high on a route when the reckoning comes, and that is a tough time to be forced to learn to climb an off-width crack or a slab or a severe overhang. It's better to learn these unique movement styles on a single-pitch climb or

Chimneys offer an intuitive movement style, but they can be scary and difficult to protect. Learning to focus and climb is crucial.

a boulder problem, not when your entire team is exposed.

Protection. Protection ratings are also part of researching a climb. PG–13-, R-, and X-rated pitches are seriously dangerous obstacles. If you've never experienced challenges like these before, a multipitch climb is not the best place to learn.

Protection Rating	What That Means	What That Means in Multipitch
G	Protection can be found every body length, and rock quality is such that all placements could hold the forces of a leader fall if placed correctly.	There is enough good gear to keep the team from creating excessive and injurious fall forces.
PG	Protection can be found every body length, but some of it might require smaller, weaker, and less secure placements. Or there are good placements but they might be less frequent than a G-rated climb.	You may need specialized equipment on your rack, or you may need to be prepared to take larger falls and possibly subject your anchor to severe fall forces.
PG-13	There are measurable sections where larger falls are possible due to less-frequent protection or lower-quality placements.	Depending on where those falls happen, the leader could be injured, or the anchor could be severely loaded.

Protection Rating	What That Means	What That Means in Multipitch
R	There are significant gaps between protection points, and a fall at certain points on a pitch could result in injury or death due to ground or ledge fall.	If the leader were to fall at certain points on a lead, a multistage small-teams rescue would be necessitated by the resulting injuries.
X-Rated	A fall at any point on a lead would likely result in injury or death.	An injured or dead partner creates a serious problem for the uninjured partner. Giant unprotected falls that load the anchor create the kinds of forces that could create sequential failures of small or marginal anchor components.

If we're uncertain about our capabilities, there are ways to gather more evidence. Lower grades, shorter climbs, and sound recommendations from a trusted climber can help us pinpoint capabilities that might be difficult to ascertain through self-reflection. If there is something about your selected climb that you have never done before, or you've done it before and had a negative experience, consider that a reason to table your heart's desire until the probabilities of success are stacked more heavily in your favor.

Assembling Your Climbing Team

All the questions you've asked of yourself must also be asked of your climbing partner, and most of the time, you know the answer to the questions before you ask them. Climbing partnerships are not like ISO ads, even if they start off that way. A climbing partnership becomes increasingly intimate in time, and it is a unique relationship. Some partnerships are romantic; some are platonic. But many valuable and functional partnerships are neither romantic nor platonic. They are forged in travail, interdependence, and the repeated affirmation of the value of life and life fully lived.

A reunion of aged climbing partners has been more than once mistaken for a reunion of veterans of foreign wars. Old companions of this sort can be politically diametric, personally vindictive, or individually inward and reticent, but the climbing bond seals their fate. They will never not be climbing partners.

Much has been written about finding climbing partners and how the right syncopation between two

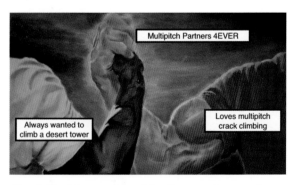

Good climbing partnerships forge unique and intimate bonds.

I have a great climbing partner out there named Cole Casserly. Cole and I have only teamed up a few times, even though he is always eager to go. I am usually the one who can't commit to a climb. Sometimes I worry about Cole getting the impression that I don't like him or that I don't respect his climbing ability. The exact opposite is true. I respect Cole immensely. I've noticed Cole since he was a kid crushing gym climbs in Charlotte. He's a gifted free climber, and I think he is a much better climber than I am. So, for me, Cole fits in a unique niche among climbing partners. He inspires me to climb my very best, and I only want to climb with him when I feel like I have my very best to offer. If I don't, if I can't come correct to the partnership, Cole does not stand out among the myriad array of partners that might pair better with my typical mediocrity. Pairing the right partner with the right objective might mean that Cole and I only do a handful of climbs in our lives together, but for me those climbs will represent occasions when I was feeling good enough to climb with Cole. I wouldn't want our partnership to be defined by the days that I held us back. I have plenty of partners to rely on for those kinds of days. —RF

people is vital for climbing. We agree, but there is not a dearth of partners out there, as many claim. In fact, there are more climbers out there than ever before. It's just that every potential partner out there might not pair with every potential objective. We believe any two people can be climbing partners, but pairs of partners should use the capabilities of their partnership to select their objectives. That's where the mix can get dysfunctional, even toxic.

If partners are not equally skilled or compatibly motivated to achieve an objective, the partnership itself will likely be one of many emergent obstacles. You might only be compatible with some partners in the gym, and only for an hour or so. You might only sync up with some partners for bouldering or sport or training, and so forth. So for any one of thousands of potential partners out there, a smaller subset of those partners might be multipitch partners. An even smaller subset of that subset might be appropriate for the climb you have in mind, and you might not have a good partner for your climb in your current retinue. You might have to go find the relationship that doesn't currently exist.

FINDING A PARTNER

There are a few dozen different ways to find a climbing partner, from Facebook forums to meet-ups, sign-up boards, flyers, and Craigslist. However a person normally goes about meeting other people, one can also go about meeting other climbers.

Your initial introduction to a new climbing partner should only be the first step. Ideally, there are three. To make this process as efficient and as effective as possible, you'll need to be patient, you'll need to be honest and forthcoming, and you'll need to be systematic.

Step 1: In Search Of. It's important for you to offer full disclosure to your pool of potential partners. It's not enough to say something vaguely inviting like "looking for a climbing partner who climbs 5.10" when you're actually looking for someone to climb

I've always been a fan of the old-school way to meet climbers. I go to where the climbers are that are doing the thing that I want to do. My goal for the outing is to meet other climbers, so I don't really have an agenda to climb. I introduce myself and then I offer to spot, belay, share snacks, whatever offering initiates more interaction. I've always enjoyed meeting people, but I feel the same nervousness and social anxiety that anybody would. Climbing can be scary, and so can meeting new people. You just have to swallow your fear, open your mind, put on a smile, and get right in there. —RF

Between social media and email, it's easier than ever to find a climbing partner. Finding a specific partner for a specific objective is where things get tricky.

the Diamond on Longs Peak. Instead, be specific: "Looking for a partner to swing on-sight leads on the Casual Route (IV 5.10a) of the Diamond on Longs Peak." The specificity of your request will deter or encourage; less capable partners won't be misled, and capable partners will be enthused by the opportunity.

Step 2: Partner Training. Once you've met that potential someone, it's folly to dive right into the objective you have in mind, no matter how modest it seems. You need to train your partner to climb with you, and your partner needs to train you to climb with them. You'd be surprised how many little idiosyncrasies we all carry with us, and discovering these little quirks is time-consuming. Spend that time on a training climb so that it doesn't detract from your intended objective.

Your training climb should be a full step down from the commitment and severity of your desired climb. For example, if you want to climb Moby Grape (III 5.8) on Cannon Cliff in New Hampshire, your training climb should be something like Thin Air (II 5.6) on Cathedral Ledge. Your training climb should let you align with your partner on a few crucial variations in the ways all partners climb with each other.

Your partner-training outing should align your climbing team. Or it should give the team some clear signals about whether or not they need more training time together. Teams that tackle an objective without alignment on these issues end up having interpersonal challenges at a time when the team needs optimal performance. It reduces the margin of error on the objective, and even if the team succeeds, misalignments sour the climbing for the whole team.

Step 3: Advanced Partner Training. Once you've aligned with your partner on a training climb,

Partner Training Checklist

Question	Alignment Solutions	Deal Breakers
Racking: Rack on the harness? Rack on a sling? Over-rack? Under-rack?	You can easily align on the style of racking (on a sling or a harness) or you can re-rack for individual leads.	You must align on the size of the rack. Some leaders like too much gear, and some like the challenge of problem-solving too little gear.
Belaying: Which device? Level of attentiveness?	You can easily align on which belay device to use. It's fair for a leader to want to be belayed by the device of her choice. Similarly, it's fair for a second to want to be belayed by a device of his choice. It's also fair for a climber to insist on the level of attentiveness his belayer demonstrates.	If your belayer is not proficient with the use of the device of your choice and unwilling to learn, you're incompatible. If your belayer is not attentive enough to make you feel comfortable, you're incompatible.
Communication: What words? Names in commands? Radios? Nonverbal communication?	You can easily align on the words you use, the use of radio, and/or the use of nonverbal communication strategies.	If there is a severe language barrier, it will be difficult to do things that require (or could require) lots of communication.

Question	Alignment Solutions	Deal Breakers
Seriousness: When is joking acceptable? When is joking unacceptable?	You should be able to align on seriousness. Some people don't like to joke around or to distract the climb with casual conversation. Some people do. Decide how serious you're going to act on the climb.	If you can't shift your seriousness to meet your partner, or vice-versa, you are dismally incompatible. You will not like each other, and you will not like the climb.
Suffering: What conditions are ideal? What conditions are unreasonable?	You should be able to decide how much you're willing to suffer together. Some people have no capacity for suffering. Some have an unhealthy amount.	If you can't shift your tolerance for suffering to meet your partner, or vice-versa, you are incompatible. One of you will be disappointed with the climb, and you'll end up disappointed with each other too.
Distractions: Dogs? Children? Cell phones? Crowds? Smoking?	Every climber tows along potential distractions and every climber has different tolerances for these distractions. Discuss and decide what you are willing to add to the challenges of the climb and what you are not.	If you can't shift your tolerance for distractions to meet your partner, or vice-versa, you are incompatible. One of you will be annoyed all day, and the other will be annoyed by the annoyance.

Partner Chart

Partner Type	Desired Objective	Partner Training	Advanced Training
Gym partner—training	Hangboard workouts. Training alone sucks.	We'll go for a walk and talk about our goals.	I can't stand all the drill sergeant stuff. Too serious. Gonna find a new partner.
Gym partner—bouldering	Purple V8. I need someone to help me stay psyched.	Let's circuit our favorite problems.	We have different strategies. We'll come up with lots of beta together on the next V8.
Gym partner—toproping	I want to burn 20 laps every other night.	Let's do 10 laps one night to get to know each other.	He's too into socializing. I need to insist that he focuses on me when I'm climbing.
Gym partner—leading	I want to climb 5.11 consistently.	Let's warm up on 5.10 and then work a couple projects together.	She really encourages me to push a little further on tough climbs. I hope I'm encouraging her too.
Bouldering partner	I want to climb this tall V5.	Let's climb some tall V3s.	He really helped me send that project, but I'm looking for someone who likes hanging with my dog while we boulder.

Partner Chart

Partner Type	Desired Objective	Partner Training	Advanced Training
Toproping partner	I want to climb every Sunday this fall.	Let's go to the gym together.	We can both bring our kids and climb together next time.
Single-pitch sport partner	I want to send a 5.13 project.	Let's go to the gym together.	I finally sent, but she hates belaying with a Grigri, she finally revealed. I'm not comfortable with an MBD.
Single-pitch trad partner	I want to work on my weakness: leading off-width.	Let's toprope some OWs.	He really encouraged me even though I took an hour to lead 60 ft. Next time I'll bring some belay glasses for him.
Grade II partner + difficulty	Gemini Crack (II 5.8)	We'll climb some first-pitch stuff at the crag.	The climb went great, but I could tell she hated the constant sun. Next time, we'll hit a shady climb.
Grade III partner + difficulty	Moby Grape (III 5.8)	Thin Air (II 5.6)	Next time we climb, I need to turn off my cell phone and bring a few extra cams.
Grade IV partner + difficulty	Scenic Cruise (IV 5.10)	Maiden Voyage (III 5.9-)	We climbed so well. I think we could do something harder and longer if we can shave more time off Grade IVs.

you can reasonably climb the original objective you had in mind. But with new partners especially, it's good to think of this climb as advanced partner training. At the end of this outing, you'll know which aspects of your partnership require deeper alignment. If you were compromising on seriousness, maybe your partner can start to be more playful. If your partner was compromising on belaying method, maybe he or she will be more accustomed or fond of the device you insisted upon. Maybe not. Either way, you'll know if some social contract or politesse was inhibiting you from being candid with one another. A climbing partnership is not a marriage (even if you are married to your climbing partner); it's okay to go looking for other partners if you can't find harmony.

Mentors

Once in while your partner search may reveal a rare treasure. In the climbing world a good mentor is hard to find. As more and more climbers explore multipitch climbing, there are fewer and fewer mentors to be found. As we've discussed in other texts, a mentor is both willing and capable, like any partner. Unfortunately, many climbers who assume the role of mentor have far more willingness than they have capability, which can be a dangerous situation.

For example, if a climber agrees to mentor another climber, they essentially stipulate that their own abilities and expertise are sufficient to take responsibility for a less capable partner. A professional guide makes the same calculation. But a professional guide is bound by the ethics of his or her trade (and the liability that comes with those ethics) to be well trained and credentialed for the responsibility assumed. A mentor

Mentor Questionnaire

- Have you ever mentored anyone else? Can I meet them?

- If you've never mentored anyone else, does your personal experience vastly outweigh the things you want to teach me? In other words, if you are mentoring me on Grade II multipitch climbing, have you done Grade III and IV multipitch? If you are mentoring me on 5.10 climbing, have you climbed 5.11 and 5.12?

- If we get into trouble, I don't have enough experience or skill to help us get out of trouble. Are you skilled in small-teams rescue? How often do you practice those skills?

- Do you have any professional guide training or certification?

- Like any partner, do we align? Just because you are willing to teach me, can I also get along with you at the crag?

might not be bound by the norms of a profession, but they take on the same moral responsibility as a guide.

On the face of it, these obligations are clear and indisputable. However, many pseudo–mentors relish the status that accompanies mentoring and leading others when they are not physically, experientially, or morally prepared for that responsibility.

Since appropriate mentors are rare and since appropriate partnerships are vital to successful multipitch climbing, it's fair to ask a few qualifying questions of a partner that would presume to be your mentor. It's equally important to ask these questions of yourself before agreeing to mentor others.

Occasionally, a climber with experience and expertise and kindness and generosity knows that the heyday of her own free-climbing and multipitch adventures has passed. She still wants to climb, but the season has arrived for her to pass on the things that she has learned. This person is a true treasure, a true resource. But those who would presume to be this person without experience, expertise, kindness, and generosity are an indignity to the sport and they are a danger to you. They are also easy to spot because their ego and presumptuousness make them conspicuous. You have to be able to see them for what they are and not be seduced by the promise of finding a mentor. For climbers, finding a good mentor is like winning a lottery, which makes us particularly susceptible to self-delusion.

Phase 2: Research and Planning

Once you've assessed your capabilities to rule out unreasonable objectives, and once you've found a climbing partner that is aligned with your objective, you'll need to decide when to climb. Almost every climb has ideal conditions, and conversely almost every climb has nightmarish conditions. You'll want to climb during the agreeable side of that spectrum. No climb is perfect all the time, but that doesn't mean that a climb is impossible or unreasonable just because conditions are not perfect. Proper preparations and planning can accommodate all but the most unruly and inhospitable conditions.

There are four main questions to answer to discover when to climb and what preparations to make for the timing you've selected:

- What is the forecast?
- What is the aspect of the approach, the climb, and the descent?
- What will the crowds be like?
- Given the forecast, the aspect, and the crowds, at what time of day should we start?

The Forecast

Forecasting services are so precise, so multifaceted, and so relevant to multipitch climbers that it is hard to justify ignoring them. The National Oceanic and

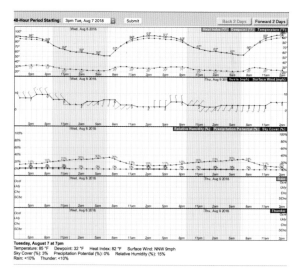

A great forecast lets the climbing team make a great plan.

	Weather Forecast Notes
High and low temperature	
Time of day for highest temperature	
Time of day for lowest temperature	
Chance of precipitation	
Time(s) of day when chance of precipitation is highest	
Type of precipitation	
Time of sunrise and sunset	
Cloud cover	
Wind direction and speed	
Chance of thunderstorm	

Atmospheric Administration, for example, provides detailed telemetry on temperature, humidity, wind speed and direction, likelihood of precipitation (of all kinds), likelihood of lightning and thunderstorms, sunrise and sunset, cloud cover, and all points trending by the day and by the hour. You'll want to make note of all those data points.

For NOAA and many other weather services, you'll need to find the closest town or weather station to your climbing venue and then select the forecast that is most proximal. For remote areas, there might not be a weather station within 10 miles. In this case you'll have to do the tedious exercise of reading multiple forecasts from stations that surround the venue.

In remote destinations the imprecision of forecasting services will enable planning but usually prompts the climbing team to plan more conservatively and for a variety of contingencies, take fewer chances with less-than-ideal forecasts, and rely heavily on continuous weather observations in field.

Aspect

What is the aspect of the approach, the climb, and the descent? It often takes some sleuthing using maps and guidebooks and route descriptions. The aspect is the directional nature of the terrain relative to the sun and cardinal directions. So in the Northern Hemisphere, if the climb faces north, it might be in the shade all day. If it faces south, it might be in the sun all day. Approaches and descents might have different aspects than the climbs themselves.

As you can imagine, aspect naturally and specifically cross-references with forecast. For example, if the approach, the climb, and the descent all face south, then I might want to avoid hot, humid, sunny, and clear forecasts. Or I might want to plan to approach, climb, and descend in the earliest and/or coolest parts of the day or when a southerly breeze is forecasted, to make the climbing more pleasant. Similarly, if the aspect is northerly, I might want to avoid cold days, especially if northerly winds are forecasted to make the climb feel even colder.

	Aspect Notes
Aspect of approach	
Aspect of climb	
Aspect of descent	

Crowds

The quality rating of a climb, calendar holidays, and local insights help the climbing team predict how many other people might have the same objective in mind that you do. Popularity is a fickle thing though. It's just as fickle for rock climbs as it is for teenagers. One day, inexplicably, climbs are mobbed with aspiring parties. The next day there isn't a soul in sight. Still, a few key predictors are the best chance you have of finding a chaotic cacophony, a congenial cohort, or absolute solitude.

The quality rating of a climb is one of most subjective, obtuse, and variable criteria that climbers can research. The quality rating rarely reveals any objective data about the rock, the difficulty, the protection, or the aesthetic quality of the climb, things that you might imagine would factor into a quality rating. There is no real consensus about any of these ratings, either. One climber's treasure is another climber's choss heap. One guidebook uses a three-star rating system, while another uses four or five.

A quality rating only predicts one thing very accurately: popularity. Local climbers and visitors alike will congregate around climbs that have higher-quality ratings, while unsung climbs remain dormant and untraveled for years. If a climb is highly regarded through quality rating, if it is considered a classic, it will attract lots of climbing parties, regardless of any objective criteria of quality or any comparable criteria on adjacent climbs. People love to climb classics.

Also, all climbs, including classics, are more popular on calendar holidays and on holidays that surround them. All climbs are more popular on weekends than weekdays. All climbs are more popular during the hours of a business day than early in the morning. Climbers, like all people, are predictably opportunistic and/or lazy in this way. A thoughtful team can plan accordingly.

Lastly, any local flashpoint, episode, or event can create predictable spikes in popularity. If a climb is featured in a commercial, television show, or movie, its popularity will spike for years afterward. Publications of guidebooks or features in climbing magazines will create popularity spikes. Lastly, the climbing community often gathers for events, service, and competitions. These gatherings are always preceded or culminated by lots of climbers coming together to do the climbs they love.

Once you've gathered your notes on forecast, aspect, and crowds, the beginnings of a logical time plan should emerge. Given all the information you've gathered, you should plan to climb at a time that is most likely to produce the experience you wish to have. It's important to note that timing will produce a certain outcome, but not all teams have the same values. Some teams want to suffer, or they want to practice suffering, so they'll pick a time for a climb that most people would consider inclement. Some teams like spending time near other people, or they enjoy

	Crowd Notes
Quality rating	
Calendar date (weekend or holiday)	
Local flashpoint (events, recent national features, new publications)	

the safety net that adjacent parties provide, so they intentionally look for crowds. Some teams enjoy the time pressures that come from imposing conditions and threatening forecasts, so they'll choose to climb when everyone else is battening down the hatches.

The point is that adequate research should result in the climbing team being less likely to be surprised or disappointed by the conditions they experience.

Phase Three: Assembling the Multipitch Kit

Once you've done all your timing research and homework, you can start to assemble the equipment that you'll need to be successful. The timing of your climb will necessitate some obvious allocations of apparel, food, water, personal comfort items, and emergency-preparedness items, and when those necessities are combined with the technical requirements of the climb, the net assemblage has to be carefully scrutinized, challenged, and revised.

Notes on Apparel

It's not easy to pick the right clothes for a multipitch climb. Manufacturers of climbing clothing would have you believe that the right collage of this season's line can perfectly equip a multipitch climber for any outing. The truth is, of course, more complex.

Apparel protects a climber from the elements and indecency, but it also inhibits or enables movement and comfort. The selected brands of climbing apparel are also much more expensive than generic athletic wear, so a consumer is tasked with reconciling an array of selection criteria including protection and

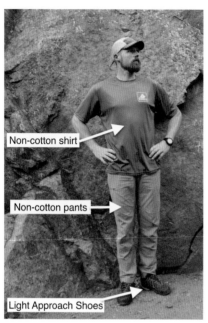

Non-cotton shirt

Non-cotton pants

Light Approach Shoes

This climber's choices for a warm day of climbing won't work for everyone, but he has a personal reason for everything he's wearing.

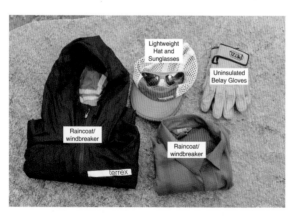

Lightweight Hat and Sunglasses

Uninsulated Belay Gloves

Raincoat/ windbreaker

terrex

Raincoat/ windbreaker

A few extras on warm days prepare the climber for sun and rain.

versatility, comfort, dexterity, fit, cost, and durability, and lastly the ethics and identity of a brand. Trying to get it right is confusing and costly.

Every climber will need protection from the elements. She'll need to stay warm when it's cold, stay dry when it's wet, stay shaded from the sun, and avoid exposure to biting insects and poisonous plants. Maybe an insulated suit of armor would do all those things, but the climber wouldn't be able to move, or she'd sweat to death or overheat. Maybe she'd wear a minimal selection of clothes and just be tough enough to deal with temperature variations and changing conditions. Like everything in climbing, you'll have to make choices, analyze and dissect the performance of those choices, and then revise and learn from every climb.

Shoes. Approaches and descents to and from multipitch rock climbs often involve a need for surefootedness on some form of 3rd- and 4th-Class terrain. If that's true, then an approach shoe with sticky

From left to right: A sturdy approach shoe for hiking in wet conditions, an approach shoe for easier climbing, and a lightweight approach shoe for up and over.

rubber outsoles proves itself as a wise choice. For many climbs, the approach shoe can also be used for lower free-climbing difficulties: one shoe for the approach, the climb, and the descent. When shoes have to be carried up the entire climb, for climbs that don't return to the base of a cliff, an approach shoe that is both nimble and lightweight stands out. But as we'll see in all categories, when a manufactured piece of equipment is more lightweight, it is also less durable, incurring more frequent replacement costs or repairs. In every case a shoe is preferable to sandals or slippers. Even if a climber becomes accustomed to approaching, climbing, and descending in sandals, a shoe will stand out if conditions change or if a climber has to run for help.

Socks. Socks don't invoke as many difficult choices. A noncotton sock that is warm enough for the forecast is advantageous because it is both warm and it wicks sweat away from a perspiring foot. A light sock when it's warm and midweight sock for colder days usually suffice, but a cold-natured person might also add a heavy sock into the mix. The length of the sock is worth exploring too. When approaches are heavily vegetated or lots of prickly vegetation is present, a longer sock that covers the ankles can offer protection. Some crack climbs necessitate the same protection over the ankles.

Undergarments. Much like socks, noncotton undergarments wick sweat away from the skin. Supportive garments are more comfortable for both men and women.

Pants and shorts. For most multipitch climbs, pants are preferable. They're more protective and versatile when conditions change, and lighter noncotton

Cotton is not always a no-no. In wide cracks and chimneys, cotton pants and shirts offer great padding and they're grippy.

fabrics can even be bearable in warmer conditions. The more pressing choice becomes how heavy the pant needs to be; cooler conditions require a heavier pant. In every case the pant should fit on the true waist so that it can be worn comfortably underneath a climbing harness. When trying pants on, stretch and high step in all directions. Make sure the fit of the pant allows for a full range of motion. Tights allow for an excellent range of motion, but they are less popular with men these days.

When conditions are swelteringly hot, shorts might be more comfortable, but even climbers in the hot and humid Southeast can tell you about shivering through an unexpected rainstorm in July. Shorts might be comfortable, but pants are more versatile. For the forecast, decide which is more important, comfort or preparedness.

Shirts. Layered noncotton shirts let a climber strip down to short sleeves during exertion, and layer up to protect from cold, sun, and insects. A collared or hooded long sleeve over a short sleeve is common and versatile.

Insulation. Vests, fleece, and puffy layers underneath wind- and rain-breaking layers keep a climber's core toasty while belaying. The layers with too much loft, or too many layers in general, can restrict movement and reach. They pull out from underneath a harness and clutter the waistline. So don't overdo it. A great puff layer can be

A micro puff layer can be worn under as insulation or slipped over everything while belaying or standing still.

worn underneath a jacket or on top of all layers while belaying.

Wind and rain layers. A light raincoat or windbreaker is common in almost all multipitch packs. If rainstorms and temperatures are forecasted to be

Warm Hat

Insulating Layer

Soft Shell Jacket

Soft Shell Pants

Full leather approach shoe

This climber's choices for a cold day of climbing allow him to take layers on and off throughout the day.

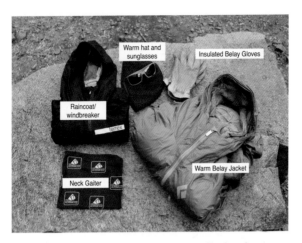

A few extras on cold days prepare the climber for standing still, covering extremities, wind, and rain.

severe, a rain pant or windbreaker pant might also accompany the jacket.

Hats, gloves, sunglasses. Hats and sunglasses shade the face and eyes from sunlight, and for many climbs they make all the difference between comfort and misery on a sunny day. Similarly, gloves that keep hands and fingers warm while rappelling and belaying are rarely resented when available, but sorely coveted when missing.

Food. Committing climbs require enough calories to sustain performance over long periods of time, and that means bringing enough food to fuel the body for hours. Energy bars, electrolyte drink mixes, energy goo, and chews all purport to provide scientifically designed nutrition for high performance. But every climber is different, and there is not a nutritional panacea out there that will work for all climbers on all climbs.

So, you're in experimentation mode with food. Find a balance of sugars and quickly metabolized energy products. Find things that are tasty that you enjoy eating because if you don't enjoy it, you probably won't make yourself eat it. Appreciate this too: Humans have been exerting themselves for centuries and we've found food that enables exertion for centuries. Most multipitch climbs don't require peak human performance, and therefore the cutting edge of nutritional science probably isn't absolutely necessary for most climbs either. In other words, don't waste your budget eating like an Olympian if a peanut butter sandwich and an apple will do.

Water. Water is an agonizing problem-solving dilemma. It's vital for life and performance and not enough of it can get dangerous quickly. But it's also heavy and bulky. You have to bring enough water, period. Hotter days with more exertion require more water. But there are often sneaky tricks to having

Collapsible water bottles are ideal for multipitch. When they're empty they don't take up much room in the backpack.

enough water without carrying so much. Are there opportunities to refill and treat water along the approach or descent? If so, you can lighten the load somewhere along the way. Can you stash water at the base of the climb and carry a small amount up with you?

Personal comforts. Every climber should develop a small collection of items that are unique to their personal comfort. Items like sunscreen, lip balm, a handkerchief, fingernail clippers, and individual hygiene and medical necessities. You will uniquely require some things and not others. No matter what these items are, a small, compact supply of them will be ideal for multipitch.

> I have always had a quirky insistence on packing a small toothbrush and toothpaste in my multipitch climbing kit. I don't like the way my mouth tastes during exertion, sweaty and acrid. I like to brush my teeth to get rid of that taste. It's one of the odd little things that I do, and I don't feel the need to apologize. It's just one of my personal comfort items. —RF

Emergency preparedness. Climbs of a committing nature, like multipitch climbs, also necessitate a state of preparedness to deal with emergencies. But when a climber starts to hypothetically consider all the potential emergencies that could occur in a remote setting or while stranded high on a multipitch climb, the supplies needed to contend with all those contingencies become unwieldy. After all, its impractical to carry an entire ambulance on every climb, but it also seems imprudent to carry nothing at all. In total a climbing team will want to consider their exposure to potential emergencies, prepare for the most likely scenarios, and then gamble on the improbability of the others.

First aid. On a long multipitch rock climb, trauma (though unlikely) is still the most likely scenario. Rockfall from above striking the climbing team, the impacts of unexpected lead falls, and unanticipated stumbles and falls are the most predictable incidents. So a first-aid kit that prioritizes traumatic emergencies is important. Sterile dressings to soak blood and apply direct pressure and cloth tape to package wounds and bind improvised splints offer a bare minimum in first-aid essentials.

The rest of a first-aid kit is usually there to deal with less severe emergencies, like minor cuts, scrapes, sprains, and illnesses. All this first-aid kit is capable of doing is providing some relief to minor incidents, and

A first aid kit this small won't do more than quickly bind a wound. Maybe that's all you need.

A medium-sized first aid kit might offer more wound and sickness solutions, but it's still minimal.

A full-sized first aid kit gives a responder more tools, but it's big and bulky.

barely stabilizing major incidents for descent, understanding that most severe incidents will require evacuation to advanced medical care.

That being said, if the team is stashing a pack, a more robust kit might stay in that larger pack, while the smaller kit is carried up a climb.

Communication device. Since the link to advanced medical care is usually central to the calculations of a multipitch team, a functional and operable communication device, one that is fully charged and functions on the climb, on the approach, and on the descent is a vital link in the chain to care for an injured partner. Cell phones, satellite communicators, radios, and satellite phones usually allow a climber to communicate with advanced medical care and SAR teams from anywhere on the planet. Finding out what works where and acquiring those tools is usually the hard part.

Bivy gear. Next to medical emergencies, a climbing team on a long objective might also want to consider its preparedness for an unplanned bivouac. Many climbers have shivered themselves through the night and calculated that an industrial garbage bag or emergency blanket would have been nice to have in the multipitch kit. Remote climbs and long climbs often expose the climbing team to unplanned overnights when the plans go awry, and on these occasions a little extra clothing, a fire-starter, an emergency blanket or bivy sack, and a little extra food is well worth its weight.

Bail gear. If a team doesn't plan for an emergency bivouac, they might instead plan for an emergency descent. They might bring any number of extra anchoring tools, cords, and rappel fixtures that allow them to improvise rappel stations along an unintended line of descent. More rappels down a longer route would of course necessitate more rappel stations, more equipment the team is willing to abandon, and a more costly descent, though many climbers have weighed the relative benefits of a half dozen rappel stations in

The Beal Escaper is an innovative tool that lets the climbing team fix their rope end but still release and retrieve their rope from below.

comparison to the value of their health and safety. In those terms there is no comparison.

Headlamp. Unplanned bivouacs and unplanned descents alike will likely expose the climbing team to sunset and the debilitating darkness. Darkness terribly inhibits a team's ability to manage rope, read terrain, and find their way home. So, a functional and charged headlamp for both team members is also a vital part of any emergency-preparedness or contingency plan.

Disposing of human waste. Next, climbers need to think carefully about the inconvenience and discomfort of an unplanned bowel movement. It's not uncommon. In fact, when a volatile digestive system is squeezed into a harness and subjected to multiple hanging belays, it is very common. Even if the team has done its best to make arrangements at the trailhead for a bowel movement, the sudden and unexpected arrival of the need to defecate is irresistible. On these occasions, a bag to contain and transport the excrement, toilet paper for tidying up, and a hand sanitizer for any necessary cleanup is well worth its weight.

Repair kit. Many climbers experience the awkward need to repair equipment or clothing unexpectedly. It's hard to imagine a team being incapacitated by a torn gear loop on a harness, or a snapped buckle on a helmet. But the ability to quickly repair these inconveniences often saves the team from wastes

Examples of Emergency-Preparedness Kits

Commitment Grade	Contents
Grade II	Light-trauma first-aid kit, light rain coat, RESTOP, hand sanitizer, communication device
Grade III (descend back to the base)	Light-trauma first-aid kit, light rain coat, RESTOP, hand sanitizer, communication device, headlamp, extra quick link and cordelette
Grade III (up and over)	Larger first-aid kit, light rain coat, RESTOP, hand sanitizer, communication device, headlamp, emergency bivy bag, repair kit
Grade IV (descend back to the base)	Larger first-aid kit, light rain coat, RESTOP, hand sanitizer, communication device, headlamp, emergency bivy bag, fire-starter, repair kit, 2 extra quick links and cordelettes, escaper
Grade IV (up and over)	Larger first-aid kit, light rain coat, light puffy jacket, RESTOP, hand sanitizer, communication device, headlamp, emergency bivy bag, fire-starter, repair kit, extra quick link and cordelette, extra energy bar

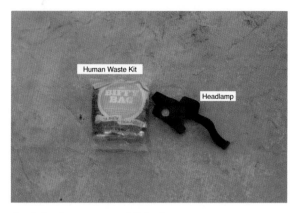

A minimal emergency kit for two common predicaments.

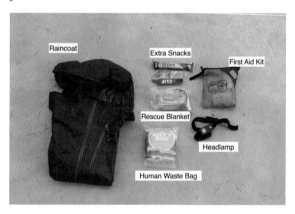

A medium-sized emergency kit might help you survive a bivouac.

of time and attention. Usually a small needle and thread accompanied by a short length of duct tape is adequate to make quick repairs to clothing and equipment and a small multitool is vital for repairing hard goods and cutting rope.

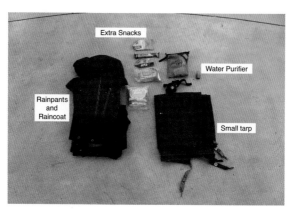

Extra Snacks

Water Purifier

Rainpants and Raincoat

Small tarp

A larger emergency kit might help you survive a more miserable bivouac.

As with any emergency preparedness, equipment selection is a wise and proactive addition to a multi-pitch kit, but all the equipment in the world is useless without some knowledge and expertise. If you don't know how to sew with needle and thread, the tiny repair kit in your pack is useless. You are not going to experiment your way to being a seamstress on the side of a cliff. So, spend some time before your climb learning to sew. Videos and tutorials on YouTube can be immensely informative and educational. If you don't have any first-aid training, your first-aid kit will be a useless decoration for your friend's injuries. Take a wilderness first-aid course, wilderness first-responder course, or educate yourself on those proficiency standards. Practice dealing with emergencies in the comfort of your home so that you'll be prepared to deal with them in adverse conditions and environments.

CHAPTER 3

Technical Equipment and Time Plans

Finally, after all the research and logistical planning, after all the emergency-preparedness and contingency planning, the climbing team gets to daydream the moves of each pitch, the rack, the anchoring and belaying gear, the rope, the toys and tools of climbing. They're so shiny.

The decision-making for equipment is just as difficult and fraught as all the other categories though, unfortunately. It takes care and deliberation. In total the climbing team is striving to distill the equipment selection down to an elegant but adequate minimum. They should not want for any equipment that could adequately protect their leads or build their anchors. Nor should they carry endless arrays of backups that merely enjoy a ride up a beautiful climb, never deployed nor utilized.

In order to make that plan and assemble that equipment, a team will need to make a careful study of the climb's topo, collate all the available beta and information about the climb, and provide themselves with a reasonable margin of error in the process.

Planning the Rack

Sitting down with a current guidebook, a web browser, and a cell phone usually equips a multipitch team with all the information they need to make an informed equipment plan for a multipitch climb. The right questions have to be asked, and the answers to those questions lead the climbing team to logical conclusions. This isn't just guesswork. In general, the team will start with an analysis of the topo to build an initial plan, they'll cross-reference that plan with online resources like MountainProject.com, SuperTopo.com, and Rockclimbing.com, and then polish off the plan with phone calls to local climbers, guides, and knowledgeable friends.

In that order the research is the least confusing. Open-source materials and locals are great for helping a team see what the topos don't indicate, like real-time changes in the route or sneaky tips that one might not find in a general description. But when these minute details dictate the planning process from the beginning, they can be misleading.

Let's plan a climb of a classic multipitch route together to see how the process might unfold.

Part One: Topo Analysis

Kor-Ingalls III 5.9. Castleton Tower. Castle Valley, Utah

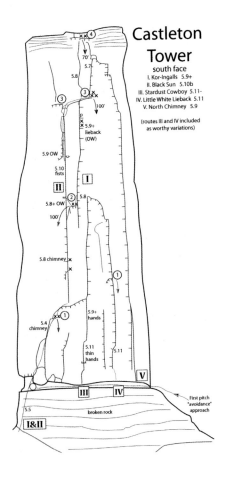

Castleton Tower
south face

I. Kor-Ingalls 5.9+
II. Black Sun 5.10b
III. Stardust Cowboy 5.11-
IV. Little White Lieback 5.11
V. North Chimney 5.9

(routes III and IV included
as worthy variations)

70'

5.7

5.8

100'

5.9+
lieback
(OW)

5.9 OW

5.10
fists

II

I

5.8

5.8+ OW

100'

5.8 chimney

5.9+
hands

5.4
chimney

5.11
thin
hands

5.11

V

First pitch
"avoidance"
approach

III

IV

5.5

broken rock

I & II

*Our entire topo analysis starts with a guidebook
description and topographic rendering like this one.*

Hopefully, before the climbing team has selected this route, they asked all the right questions and did all the research that should precede this final level of planning. Let's think through those initial steps.

Capabilities? I've climbed on sandstone near Moab, Utah, before, and I've climbed 5.9 cracks in Red Rocks and Indian Creek. I've climbed off-width and chimney features like these before, but I'm planning to do a couple days of single-pitch climbing in the area to help me get acquainted with the rock.

Partner? My partner has about the same history on this type of climbing as I do, but he has done more climbing in chimneys and wide cracks than I have. We have not climbed a desert tower before, and some friends said that we shouldn't start with the Castleton Tower, but we're both excited for this classic climb to be our first desert tower. It sounds like a good adventure to both of us.

Timing? The south-facing route is one of the most popular climbs in the world, and it's in Castle Valley. We're hoping for a day with mild daytime temperatures, little wind, and few crowds, so we're planning to start early, hit the base of the route at sunrise, and climb in the coolest part of the day before other parties arrive.

We're ready to analyze the route.

1. Is the climb an up-and-over? Or straight-up-straight-down? Or a hybrid?

Up-and-over climbs don't descend the same path that they climb. So, the team will need to bring all their equipment with them on the climb because their descent is not likely to return to the base of the climb where they started.

Straight-up-straight-down climbs climb up and then descend the same route or an immediately adjacent route. The team can stash some things at the base of the route because their descent will take them back to the place where they started.

Hybrids do some unique combination of those things. There is usually a point where the path to the climbing and the path from the descent diverge, like in a gully or drainage. The climb ascends one line via one path, descends a different line via a different path, and then eventually returns to the original fork in the path. The team can stash gear at the fork, but they'll be up and over from that point.

The Kor-Ingalls is a hybrid. We can carry packs up to the base of a little cliff band, but from there one path goes to the base of our route. We climb the south face but rappel down the opposite north face, and then we have to walk back around to our packs. That means we can bring just enough clothes, food, water, emergency-preparedness items, and personal items for the climb, but leave extras stashed in our packs. We'll need to bring our hiking shoes too, since there is a short walk from the bottom of our rappels back to our packs.

2. How do we get down? Walk-off? Rappel? Hybrid?

Walk-offs scramble or hike down a path, a gully, or a drainage in order to descend. They're nice because the descent is not technical and therefore the team isn't exposed to 5th-Class terrain if weather arrives. If the team can make it to the top, they can usually weather the descent in most conditions. The team has to be sure to bring a change of shoes though. Descending in climbing shoes can be uncomfortable.

Rappels are usually more direct lines of descent, but they are technical. The team will be exposed to 5th-Class terrain during the descent, and that is more dangerous than nontechnical descents. Even though rappel lines seem shorter, the rigging might take more time than simply walking down a slightly longer distance. Still, rappels don't require a change of shoes, and in many cases they are the best solution for descent. Rappel descents require enough rope to reach a series of fixed rappel stations, and those two requirements have to be in place for rappelling to even be an option.

Hybrids are a combination of the two styles and they usually entail the advantages and disadvantages of both. The team will likely need all three necessities to get down: a change of shoes, enough rope to rappel, and fixed rappel stations.

The Kor-Ingalls seems like an annoying hybrid. We climb up, we walk across the top of the tower, and then we rappel down the North Face. There are fixed anchors to get down, but we'll need another rope to make the rappels. So, we'll need to carry our shoes up and we'll need a second rope.

3. How long are the pitches?

Pitch lengths tell the climbing team a lot. They tell the team how much rope they'll need, how much rack they'll need, how hard it will be to bail, and how hard it will be to rescue a lead climber. When pitches exceed half a rope's length, it can be difficult to communicate, the leader will need a larger rack to protect the pitch and build an anchor, and retreat will require a second rope and/or improvised rappel stations.

For Kor-Ingalls, pitch one is 140 feet, pitch two is 100 feet, pitch three is 100 feet, and pitch four is 70 feet.

4. How much rack will we need to protect the pitches?

Most climbing teams should feel adequately protected if they place gear every body length, roughly every 5 to 6 feet. The rack calculation then unfolds quickly: If the leader leads a 60-foot pitch and places protection every 6 feet, it will take nine placements to protect the entire pitch. At first, this calculation seems odd, because it's easy to forget that the pitch starts and ends at an anchor.

For the Kor-Ingalls we have one long pitch (140 feet), one moderate pitch (100 feet), one crux pitch (100 feet each), and one exit pitch (70 feet). So if we protect the first pitch every 6 feet, we'll need twenty-two placements. That seems like a lot. Let's look at some options:

- We can carry a huge rack.

- We can place protection less frequently. Placing protection every 10 feet reduces the placement count to thirteen.

- We can split the pitches up into smaller bits. If we split the first pitch into two individual pitches, we can get down to ten placements in 6-foot increments.

60-foot pitch / placements every 6 feet = 10 – 1 placements (because the last placement is the anchor)

It's not easy to make this choice, and it is a consequential choice. If we increase the amount of equipment we carry, it will take more time to deploy it, to clean, and it will be heavy to carry, making the free climbing harder. If we space the equipment more, we are at risk of taking larger lead falls, which could increase the chance of injury. If we split the pitches up, we take extra time, which means more water and food, weight, and more exposure to the morning sun, and we'll still need enough equipment to build an anchor since there is not a permanent anchor in the middle of the first pitch.

For this climb, we're going to be a little conservative, but not too conservative. We're going to plan to place equipment every 10 to 15 feet if the free climbing doesn't feel too challenging. We'll risk the bigger falls when they are less likely. We'll just plan to slow down and climb carefully on those sections. On the harder sections, we're going to plan to place protection every 6 feet. Our protection plan will look like this:

Pitch Number	Length	Spacing	Number of Placements
1	140 feet	15 feet	8
2	100 feet	10 feet	9
3	100 feet	6 feet	15*
4	70 feet	10 feet	6

*When something in the plan stands out so drastically, like the fact that this one pitch is going to require so much gear, there is likely a sneaky trick or strategy to help. We'll keep this problem in mind as we continue the planning process.

5. What kind of protection and materials will I need to accommodate my protection plan and build anchors?

It is difficult to look at a topo and know precisely which placements to anticipate, especially when the total number of placements increases more and more. Instead, the topo can give clues as to the range of options you can anticipate, and then you can plan to be creative and versatile with your rack to make your rack go the distance. We start with protection clues. Protection clues are best guesses from topos, photos, and all the other beta available about what range of protection we can anticipate.

Protection Clues	Likely Placements
Cracks	Cracks will likely offer cam placements in that size range for their entire length. Cracks also offer occasional constrictions for stoppers, hexes, and Tricams.
Jumbled flakes and blocks	Jumbled flakes and blocks often offer a chance to place something on any rack with a wide range of sizes. There are often deepening cracks behind flakes that could take a range of cam or Tricam sizes. There are often constrictions beneath and behind blocks for a range of stoppers.
Bolts and pins	The presence of a bolt or a fixed piton usually means that it is difficult to find other protection before or after. Slings and carabiners alone might protect whole sections.

Protection Clues	Likely Placements
Faces	The protection on face climbs almost always offers a direct correlation between difficulty and size. Easier face climbs will have chunkier gaps, pockets, and horizontal cracks. They'll take medium to larger gear. Harder faces have tiny holds, small seams and cracks, and smaller protection.
Chimneys and wide cracks	These features are often so wide they have to be climbed without protection, or there are bolts, or we might discover that they present as two opposing faces, with all the corresponding opportunities of any individual face climb.

For the Kor-Ingalls, we see a few great protection clues. They'll help us look back at our protection plan and make some choices about the rack.

Pitch Number	Number of Placements	Protection Clues	Rack
1	8	Jumbled flakes and block lead to a chimney.	Cams and Tricams from 0.4 inch to 2 inches should protect the flakes and blocks and the chimney (if the chimney even has protection).
ANCHOR	Two bolts for anchor. We'll need a cordelette or double-length sling and two carabiners.		

Pitch Number	Number of Placements	Protection Clues	Rack
2	9	Two cracks	Not only one but two cracks on this pitch. The cams and Tricams from the first pitch should work here.
ANCHOR	Two bolts for anchor. We'll need a cordelette or double-length sling and two carabiners.		
3	15*	Off-width, three bolts	Three bolts means I need 12 other placements. Double rack from #4 to #6 Camalot.
ANCHOR	Two bolts for anchor. We'll need a cordelette or double-length sling and two carabiners.		
4	6	Chimney to flakes, cracks, and block	Rack from first pitch should be fine.
ANCHOR	Two bolts for anchor. We'll need a cordelette or double-length sling and two carabiners.		
Total Rack	Single set of Camalots from 0.4 to #3. Double Camalots from #4 to #6. Six alpine draws. Four shoulder-length slings with carabiners. Tricams from Pink to Purple. Two cordelettes and four extra carabiners for anchors.		

6. What will we need to belay?

Just like in single-pitch trad, it's common and prudent to belay the leader with a tool that protects the leader and the belayer from rockfall. In multipitch terrain, when the commitment and exposure are greater, these precautions are particularly advisable. An assisted braking device will provide a belayer with a margin of error in the event of rockfall from above. It will also make it more likely for the belayer to catch hard falls from hanging belays.

For the second, it's common and prudent for the leader to select a belay tool that allows her to multitask, in preparation for transition. So an auto-blocking- or plaquette-style belay tool is a great choice.

For the Kor-Ingalls, we'll plan to belay the leader with a Petzl Grigri 2, and the second with an ATC Guide.

7. What will we need for the free climbing?

In all the preparations of equipment, rack, and rope, don't forget that you actually have to free-climb as well. Most climbs require a unique combination of free-climbing-related accessories and the right climbing shoes.

For the Kor-Ingalls, we'll plan to use a full tape job on the hands and fists, long sleeves for the off-width and chimney sections, chalk, and a flat-lasted comfortable climbing shoe.

8. What will we need to descend?

We've already mentioned the requirements of descent, but it figures into the topo analysis as well. We do the same kind of analysis of a descent as we do for an ascent. How many ropes will be needed to reach rappel stations? What rappel device will we need? What personal anchor systems and backups will we use?

For the Kor-Ingalls, we do three rappels down the North Face. We'll need a second rope. We'll need an anchor at each set of rings, personal tethers and extensions for the rappels, and two ATCs. So the climbing rack will need to be supplemented with an additional double-length sling, and an additional ATC Guide.

9. What if we need to bail?

It's important to look at a topo and imagine what bailing would look like at any point in the climbing. What would it look like if the team needed to bail in the middle of leading a pitch? What would it look like if the team needed to bail in the middle of seconding a pitch? Where are the fixed anchors and how would the team get to them?

For the Kor-Ingalls, we can lower the leader to the ground or the belay from all pitches except the top of the first pitch. We can also descend the route from one bolted anchor to the next if we need to bail.

10. How long will this take?

Teams should be able estimate how long a climb will take, and that time plan also factors in to the start time, just as much as the weather and the crowds. Time plans should be padded with generous margins of error, especially on new climbs. Professional guides train to lead all pitches at approximately 10 feet per minute. But professional guides are rarely challenged by the free climbing or the protection. They move efficiently to provide time for their clients to enjoy the climbing. For most climbers, it's possible to climb as fast as a guide on less challenging terrain with obvious protection placements, or on terrain that is familiar. When the climbing is unfamiliar, challenging, and difficult to protect, we all climb more carefully, more deliberately, and more slowly. Calculating a much slower rate is the way to go to create an accurate time plan.

For the Kor-Ingalls, our time plan might look like this:

Part of Climb	Time Allotted	Margin of Error
Approach	40 min.	100%. In case we get lost. +/− 40 min.
Prep for climb	10 min.	0%. We're going to get ready and climb. No stalling.
First pitch	140 ft. / 10 ft. per min. = 14 min. to lead. 14 min. to second. 28 min. total.	50%. We might get off-route or slowly adjust to the climbing. +/− 14 min.
Transition	5 min.	0%. We don't mess up transitions.
Second pitch	100 ft. / 10 ft. per min. = 10 min. to lead. 10 min. to second. 20 min. total.	50%. We might get off-route or slowly adjust to the climbing. +/− 10 min.
Transition	10 min. We're going to rest a little before the crux pitch.	0%. We don't mess up transitions.
Third pitch	100 ft. / 5 ft. per minute = 20 min. to lead. 20 min. to second. 40 min. total.	100%. We're not going to underestimate this pitch. It might take us twice as long as we think. +/− 40 min.

Part of Climb	Time Allotted	Margin of Error
Transition	5 min.	0%. We don't mess up transitions.
Fourth pitch	70 ft. / 10 ft. per min. = 7 min. to lead. 7 min. to second. 14 min. total.	50%. We might get off-route or slowly adjust to the climbing. +/− 7 min.
SUMMIT CELEBRATION	30 min. Selfies, snacks, yodeling.	100%. We might hang out longer or not at all if we need to leave. +/− 30 min.
Transition to rappel	5 min.	0%. We don't mess up transitions.
Rappel 1	5 min.	0%. We don't mess up rappelling.
Transition	5 min.	1,000%. We've heard people get their ropes stuck when they pull, once in a while. +/− 50 min.
Rappel 2	5 min.	0%. We don't mess up rappelling.
Transition	5 min.	1,000%. We've heard people get their ropes stuck when they pull, once in a while. +/− 50 min.
Rappel 3	5 min.	0%. We don't mess up rappelling.
Transition	5 min.	1,000%. We've heard people get their ropes stuck when they pull, once in a while. +/− 50 min.
Hike to pack and repack	5 min.	0%. We don't mess up repacking.

Part of Climb	Time Allotted	Margin of Error
Hike out	40 min.	50%. Downhill is usually faster unless we get lost. +/− 20 min.
Totals	Estimated time: 4 hr. 42 min.	Maximum time: 8 hr. 58 min.

Part Two: Study Open-Source Sites Online

When a team does the work of a topo analysis, equipment and rack planning, and time planning, they have a better sense of what they are looking for when they read open-source commentary on the internet. It's difficult to put open-source commentary into perspective when climbs are unfamiliar and there is uncertainty. Commenters almost always announce their opinions in a definitive and authoritative way,

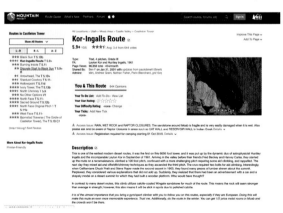

MountainProject.com is a difficult place to start one's research because the information there is often contradictory.

and it's tempting to read those comments as absolute truth. Some of them are, some of them are not. Sometimes the comment was true when it was written, but the climb or the features on the climb have since changed, rendering the comment obsolete.

Surveying online commentary really only serves one purpose: It adds depth and nuance to a plan. So much of any route plan involves best guesses and clues. Online commentary, especially photos, helps add more clarity to the mystery.

For the Kor-Ingalls, for example, the Mountain Project.com entry shows dozens of photos of the crux of the route and photos of every other pitch too. We can see the racks used by other teams, the size and length of the crux crack. We can feel confident about our racking choices, or revise them based on the evidence we learn there. I also read conflicting information about the rappels. Some say I can get down with one 70m rope; some say I need two 60m ropes. Some say rap back down the Kor-Ingalls. Some say rap the North Face.

Most important, before we do the last part of our research, calling locals and guides, we want to be well prepared to talk to them, and we want to be respectful of their time. The questions that we want to reserve for them are the questions that we cannot otherwise answer from research and study.

Part Three: Call a Local or a Guide

When you call a local or a guide, you are cashing in an exclusive favor. It's amazing how generous these folks are with their expertise and their time; all the more reason not to abuse their generosity. When you call a guide or a local, you are calling to solve lingering mysteries that your research has not revealed, or receive some affirmation that your plan is a good plan. You can't do that if you haven't done your homework, and it's especially insulting to these people to ask them to do all your homework for you.

For the Kor-Ingalls route, I really only have two questions for a guide. I'm curious about those rappels. It would be nice not to carry that second rope, and I'm more than happy to manage a 70m of rope instead of 120m, even if I have to do extra rappels on the way down. I'm also curious about the crux. I'm planning to carry a lot of extra rack for that pitch (double cams from #4 to #6), if I can get protection deep in the off-width or in the chimney, then I could maybe slim the rack down to singles.

When you are well prepared to talk to a guide or a local, they will respect your initiative and your investment in the places and the climbs that they love. Plus, the specificity of your question is easy to answer efficiently.

Backpack

Finally, after all this research and planning, I've got the kit that I think is just right. I've got the rope and rack just right. I need to decide who carries what up the route and how. There are three main options: individual carrying, muling, and hauling.

Individual carrying means that my partner and I each carry all the things that we individually need and we split up the team gear. Each individual carries her own extra clothes, personal comfort items, food and water, and shoes. A small backpack or fanny pack

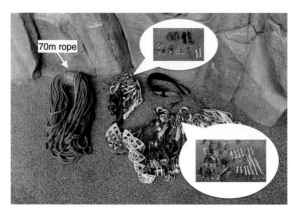

70m rope

The photo of a team's entire climbing kit is almost ubiquitous in climbing. This team is heading up the Kor-Ingalls route on Castleton Tower (III 5.9+).

usually does the trick. The team splits up any group gear. Extra rope, extra rack, first-aid kit, etc., are equitably divided.

Muling is when the second—the climber that gets to enjoy a toprope—carries everything except the

On some climbs, the climber and belayer will each carry their own shoes, water, and extras.

rack. All the extra stuff (shoes, food and water, first aid, extra rope, personal items) goes in one backpack, and the second becomes a mule . . . a rock-climbing mule.

Hauling is when the lead trails a

This team has packed to carry their equipment individually.

This team is having the second become a mule.

This team has decided to carry individual packs, but in the chimney sections, they will dangle the packs underneath each climber.

second line to haul up the extra backpack. No one has to rock-climb with a backpack on, but the leader has to haul the pack.

For the Kor-Ingalls, we're going to make the second climber be the mule on pitches 1, 2, and 4. But we're going to haul that pack on the wide crux pitch.

Notes

You will have taken so many notes to prepare for your climb: notes on weather, a point-by-point time plan, a weather forecast, a topo analysis. Take it all with you, and take notes along the way. These notes will come in handy on the climb, and they will also serve as reference if you ever return to this climb.

Photo copies of the climbing topo, hand written notes, and a tiny field notebook used to be the way to capture information about a climb

Generations of climbers used a climber's notebook for these notes. But these days a modern smartphone can capture these documents in a way that can be instantly shared with a climbing partner's phone.

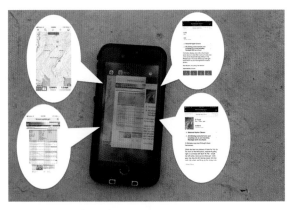

A smart phone can snap photos of guidebook pages, images from the internet, map images and coordinates., a real time track of one's progress on approach. It's an amazing note taking tool.

CHAPTER 4

Climbing a Multipitch Climb

Having made such careful preparations, executing a multipitch rock climb should be a joyous and worthwhile adventure. As we can imagine though, just as the planning and preparation for a multipitch climb is more rigorous and more vital, the execution is more complicated and requires greater care and precision. In single pitch the terrain will forgive us for sloppiness most of the time. In all but the worst-case scenarios, we can lower to the ground, leave some equipment behind, and walk away with a lesson to reflect upon.

In multipitch, sloppiness, imprecision, and a lack of skill can strand a party in 5th-Class terrain, drastically alter time plans, expose the team to inclement weather, or clog up popular routes with incompetent rope teams that would be better served by honing their skills in more forgiving terrain. In other words, multipitch climbing should be about skillfully executing a thoughtful plan. Many of the "epics" that climbing teams endure are directly attributable to a lack of planning, a lack of skill/competence, or the interference of an unforeseen agent (like unprepared and unskilled parties).

If all goes well, all multipitch climbs should smoothly cycle the following sequence of events:

Approach

- Team hikes in with a carefully prepared and double checked kit, following a careful time plan.
- Team finds climb.
- Team set up the rope, rack, and kit for climbing.

Climbing

- The leader leads the first pitch.
- The leader anchors, sets off belay, pulls up all the extra rope.
- The leader hauls (if necessary).
- The leader belays the second.
- The second cleans the pitch.

Transitions

- The second anchors.
- The team prepares the leader the rope and the rack for the next pitch.
- Once the leader is on belay, the next pitch begins.
- This process is repeated for the entire climb.

Descent

- The team walks off the top or.
- The team begins a multistaged rappel.
- The team hikes out.

A basic multipitch climbing sequence has six distinct skill blocks:

1. Approaching efficiently and finding the climb
2. Leading the pitches (and lead belaying) and anchoring
3. Seconding the pitches (and belaying the second)
4. Transitions from one pitch to the next
5. Transitions from going up to going down
6. Descending (multistage rappelling or walking off or some combination thereof)

Additionally, there are skills if all does not go well, but we'll focus on those skills later in the text. For now, let's examine the six skill blocks for a well-executed multipitch climb.

Approach Efficiently and Find the Climb

After years and years of reading about climbs, researching them, and driving down obscure dirt roads looking for obscure trailheads, the skill of approaching and finding a climb becomes inexplicably familiar. Experienced climbers are doing things that they are not even consciously aware of to find their destinations. Some of those reflexive skills can be quantified and learned more rapidly; some just require a prerequisite number of failures, trial and error, and occasional dumb luck.

To start, guidebooks, open-source online resources, and locals and guides offer the same preparatory resources for finding the approach and then the climb as they do for details about the climb itself. If you've done your homework, most approaches are just a matter of connecting geographic dots, paying attention to signage, and following directions. There are few key skills that are unique to finding rock climbs, and we'll cover those in this chapter. Climbers like to pretend that they divine their way to climbs, like a mystic rock hound, but the truth is that they've learned to pay attention to some conspicuous patterns, whether they are conscious of those patterns or not. In addition to doing your research and following directions, you'll also want to hone three main skills: heads-up hiking, distinguishing a climber trail from a hiker trail, and following climber signs.

Heads-up hiking. Climbers learn to hone a continuous instinct to lift their eyes up from the mini-obstacles and steps along a path to continuously survey the terrain around them. It's a skill that you don't realize you're doing unless someone makes you aware of it. Climbers are paying attention to the lay of terrain, how terrain funnels into drainages, rises to ridges, or flattens in plateau. They pay attention to aspect, perking up when aspects align with their objective. If the climb they seek is north-facing, then any north-facing aspect along the approach could feel like the climb is going to feel. They learn to look ahead and average out all the twists and turns and switchbacks in a trail system. Switchbacks can be especially bewildering if a climber isn't able to heads-up hike. If a traveler is staring at a compass, a long switchback will seem as if it is carrying the traveler away from an intended destination. A heads-up hiker, like a good climber, perceives the net result of switchbacks and their lazy zigzagging turns, defying a single cardinal direction in any moment but achieving that direction in aggregate.

When approaching, keep a close eye on how the terrain continually converges on your objective. If your approach is not approaching, you might be on the wrong path.

Mostly, it's important to keep an eye on the climb, the main feature, as you approach. For dramatic and conspicuous features, like Castleton Tower from the previous chapter, it will be easier. In more densely wooded areas, the glimpses might be more fleeting, through foliage or occasional clearings. Every approach generally converges on the objective. If you are not closing in the on the objective, distracting switchbacks and micro-detours aside, you are probably not going the right way.

Distinguishing a climber trail from a hiker trail. You'll want to learn to distinguish a climber's trail from a hiker's trail. In a formal sense, hiker trails are usually official, officially maintained, officially marked on maps, officially signed and demarcated. Climber trails almost always leave the main trail, leave the hiking and plodding masses, to scurry off to a more clandestine terminus. That being said, climbers aren't rabbits. We have our own mass, our own girth, and our own impact on ground soil and vegetation. When dozens of climbers, day after day, turn off of a main trail, our paths are more subtle than the pedestrian highways carved by land managers, but they are clearly made by human feet. Don't go chasing animal paths, and don't get paranoid; a climber path

Some climber paths are clearly marked.

Sometimes the indications of a climber path are more subtle: a cairn, an approach shoe footprint, climbing shoe rubber scums.

has recognizably human indications. Climbers like to communicate insider detours to one another by using cairns and other subtle signs.

Climber signs. A climber trail can be confirmed by looking closely at our footprints. The dot-rubber of climbing approach shoes is easy to distinguish from any other sneaker or hiking shoe, and it's often the telltale distinction between a climber path and Boy Scouts heading off-piste. Similarly, the scum of climbing-shoe rubber is unmistakable. On many approaches, climbers turn off the main trail by marching up an indicated slab or rock step, and black smears of their approach shoes are a good sign that you are traveling where other climbers have traveled before. Lastly, it's sad but predictable: Our trash is unique. When climbers accidentally spill their chalk bags, it's hard to mistake those chalky crumbles for anything other than the sign of a climber. Similarly, our energy bar wrappers, our colorful tape markers, labels from our rope ends, and equipment stashed by other climbers can be found at the base of most crags. They're a good sign that you're where you want to be, and you can do the resource a service and pick up the trash once you've found your way.

Once you're in the general vicinity of your climb, tracing along the base of cliff, you can start to pick out micro features that indicate the start of your climb, but don't forget about all the other signs. Repeated parties of climbers stomp out a recognizable patch at the base of a climb; there tends to be small signs of their presence like shoe scum and chalked handholds. It's almost always the coincidence of these signs that help the climbing team distinguish an established climb from something that might be a climb one day.

Once you've found the start of your climb, it's wise to confirm the starts of the neighboring climbs too. Usually, that's a clear confirmation that you've actually found your climb. If the climb you're looking at seems to reflect the indications of your topo, the climbs beside it should be reflected on the adjacent topos as well.

Getting Ready to Lead the First Pitch

The ritual of beginning a multipitch is not unlike the ritual of beginning a single-pitch climb: The leader racks up, the rope is flaked into a neat pile on the belayer's brake-hand side, the leader ties in to the rope on the top side of the rope stack.

For multipitch, the second only does a couple things differently than single pitch. The second should

The rope is stacked neatly on the belayer's brake-hand side, and the belayer is already tied in to the other side of the rope.

Small critters will chew through packs to reach extra food. Or they chew up salt-sweaty straps and apparel. Stow it all away. Suspended packs are the best defense against these marauding rodents.

go ahead and tie in the bottom side of the rope. Unlike single pitch, the belayer is definitely going to climb up behind the leader, and there is a special need for efficiency. So tying the second climber in eliminates delays and guarantees that the leader won't be able to pull the end of the rope up the cliff without his second on the other end of it.

Additionally, the second and the leader can either stow away or pack up all the rest of their multipitch-climbing equipment so that as soon as the second is on belay, he can begin climbing.

Leading the Pitch and Belaying the Leader

An experienced single-pitch leader should be able to reflexively lead any pitch of a multipitch climb; that is especially true of the first pitch. On the first pitch, the leader uses protection, an effective belay, and

Falling directly onto the belayer, a factor 2 fall, creates painful and destructive impact forces on the climber, the belayer, and the anchor.

Discussions of fall factors are often overheard at single-pitch crags around the country, and it's great that climbers are discussing this concept. It's important to note, however, that fall factors are a useless calculation in single-pitch climbing because a climber can't fall farther than the amount of rope in the system. They'll just hit the ground. All fall factors in single pitch will necessarily be less than 1.

Remember, a fall factor is calculated by the length of a fall divided by the amount of rope in the system.

Fall factor = fall distance / amount of rope in the system

So multipitch climbing can create the kinds of falls where a fall factor can exceed 1. In other words, it's possible for the leader to fall past the belayer. Fall factors that exceed 1 create uncomfortably large forces on the lead climber, on the belayer, and on the anchor, especially as the leader begins to converge on a fall factor of 2, the highest possible fall factor.

free-climbing ability to ultimately prevent groundfall, just like in single pitch. In multipitch, just like in single pitch, the leader should have concern for the seconding climber on traverses and overhangs, care to prevent rockfall or at least announce rockfall when it happens, and clear communication skills.

After the first pitch, as the team gets farther and farther from the ground, the leader will need to think more carefully about how to protect themselves off the belay and how to protect the belayer from the forces of lead fall.

Leading the second pitch will be less familiar to an experienced single-pitch climber than leading the first. There are three main options for the leader to consider, and the nature of the anchor, the terrain above and below the anchor, and the capabilities of the belayer will help dictate which of those options is just right.

Leading off a big ledge. If the belayer is anchored on a large ledge, a ledge so large that it will likely be impacted if the leader were to fall, the arrangement of the lead belay is similar to belaying off the ground. The leader won't be able to create a fall factor greater than 1 because he will hit the ledge before any fall distance can exceed the amount of rope in the system. In this arrangement the leader will want to protect the pitch from ledge-fall, not groundfall.

Leading off a big ledge is like leading off the ground, especially if the ledge is too big to fall past.

Clipping the anchor as the first piece. If the belayer is at a hanging stance, the leader can clip the shelf or a strong component of the anchor as the first piece. In this arrangement it will be difficult to fully create a fall factor of 2, and each protection placement the leader places further decreases the severity of a lead fall. If he does fall, the belayer's counterweight will be powerfully loaded. The belayer will likely be displaced a great distance. Unlike catching falls in single-pitch terrain, in multipitch the belayer will be tied to the anchor, so it's difficult to catch falls the way we're accustomed to. Instead, any upward displacement will be immediately halted by the connection to the anchor, which can be abrupt and jarring. It's worth practicing this catch in a single-pitch setting once or twice.

This arrangement has the benefit of feeling familiar to most belayers. Also, if the leader needs rope tension to rest on the climbing rope, it's easier to effect that tension with the benefit of a counterweight (like the belayer's body).

Direct belay of a leader. If the team needs to protect the belayer from upward displacement, an awkward displacement, or if protection is unavailable immediately after the belay, a direct belay is a viable option. Direct belays are not common in the United States, but just because something is unfamiliar doesn't mean that it has no value, or that it is somehow dispensable. Direct belays transfer the force of lead fall directly onto an anchor, and therefore only result in minimal displacement of the belayer.

Fixed point rigging should minimize vertical displacement.

Second bolt acts purely as a backup.

The rigging of direct belay for a leader creates a redundant connection point for a Munter hitch, with as little vertical travel as possible.

The belayer pulls slack down out of the Munter hitch, and a slightly sagging loop travels up to the leader. It takes practice.

The belayer must maintain the brake to catch the fall.

Leader falls load the fixed point, not the belayer's body.

When the leader falls, the belayer must keep a firm grip on the brake strand.

The force of the leader's fall to relays the fixed point, not the belayer's body.

Catching a lead fall with a fixed point belay doesn't yank the belayer into the anchor.

Vertical displacement of this belayer will bonk straight into the low roof overhead. It's a good time for a direct belay.

Traverses are awkward to catch because the belayer gets wrenched sideways. Another good time for a direct belay.

Leading and Belaying a Leader in Multipitch	Advantages	Disadvantages	Logical Times to Apply
Belayer belays the leader off of body weight. The leader does not clip the anchor as the first piece.	Efficient, and the distance between the belayer and first protection point creates a more natural catch.	In hanging belays or when leading off of narrow stances, the leader can create a fall factor of 2, the most severe fall possible.	It's logical to do this off the ground or off of a ledge that is so large it's just like the ground.
Belayer belays the leader off of body. Leader clips the anchor as the first piece.	It is unlikely to create a fall factor of 2. The belayer can provide tension to the leader using counterweight. This belay style feels familiar.	Catching large falls in this arrangement is difficult and jarring. Counterweight arrangements could necessitate a belay escape if there is an emergency.	Most of the time teams apply this technique. It is especially well suited when there is adequate protection, falls will likely be shorter, and the leader will likely need some support from the belayer.
Direct belay of a leader.	Lead fall forces are transferred directly to the anchor instead of the belayer's counterweight. Easier to catch falls, especially large falls and higher fall factors.	If the team is not practiced in the technique, it can be dangerously misapplied. It is difficult to apply this technique to anchors with removable components; it's best applied to bolt anchors.	Teams apply this if displacing the belayer could be hazardous (low roofs), if the climbing traverses off the belay, if there is not adequate protection off the belay, and if fall factor 2 is more likely.

Anchoring

When a leader nears the end of an indicated pitch, the immediate chore will be constructing an anchor and connecting to that anchor with a clove hitch.

The clove hitch is easily adjustable, quick to tie, and quick to untie. It provides excellent security to the climber.

As the leader arrives, she builds an anchor, connects to it with a clove hitch and locking carabiner, and calls "off belay."

We'll discuss anchoring more in the next chapter, but for now let's imagine a familiar anchoring sequence on a pair of bolts. When anchor components are really strong, like bolts, a self-adjusting anchoring system, like the quad, is often a logical choice. The leader constructs the anchor, connects to the masterpoint with a clove hitch, and calls "off belay."

Belaying the second. The leader has a few main chores when belaying the second. First, she must pull up all the rope and then establish the belay. Second, she must belay attentively and effectively. Third, she must multitask while belaying to care for her own personal needs (water, food, clothing, etc). Fourth, she must prepare the rack and rope for transition.

As the second arrives at the anchor, she must choose where to position herself to expedite transition. We'll look closely at transition variations.

Swinging leads. The second becomes the leader. In this transition the second should arrive on the same

If your team is swinging leads, get the rack ready to hand off to the second while you belay.

Belaying the Second and Direct Belays

When belaying a second, the direct belay is the most prudent option. Belaying the second directly off the anchor usually creates the least overall load on the anchor, and it keeps the belayer from trapping his own

Ways to Belay the Second	Quickly Converts to Lowering	Allows the Belayer to Provide Slack Quickly	Provides the Belayer with a Margin of Error
Direct Belay: Munter	Yes	Yes	No
Direct Belay: One-Way Munter	No	No	Yes
Direct Belay: Grigri	Yes	Yes	Yes
Direct Belay: Auto-blocking Belay Device	No	No	Yes
Redirected Counterweight	Yes	Yes	No

body weight in the system. And adding auto-blocking and assisted braking devices also gives the belayer a margin of error if anything were to incapacitate the belayer.

Smooth and Comfortable for Me to Use	Allows the Belayer to Quickly Create a Raising System	Keeps the Belayer Out of the System
Yes	No	Yes
Yes*	Yes	Yes
Yes	Yes	Yes
Yes*	Yes	Yes
No	No	No

* Any tool that binds or traps the brake strand, like an auto-blocking belay device or a one-way Munter, creates more friction than alternative techniques. It's not the most arduous task to pull in slack, but it does require more work than an assisted braking device like a Grigri.

Any ledge, even a tiny ledge, will let the leader stack the rope. Rope stacks are efficient and easy to manage.

Larger ledges allow the belayer to stack the rope neatly and quickly.

Lap coils are more time-consuming to prepare than a rope stack, and they require careful management, but in a hanging stance there is really no better way to do it.

When direct belaying a second climber, it's still important to use a fundamentally sound belay technique.

- Leading the next pitch
- Clove hitch to the right of the belayer
- Pitch climbs in this direction

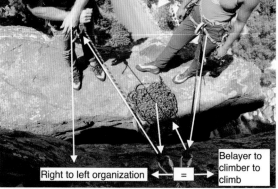

- Right to left organization
- =
- Belayer to climber to climb

If the second is about to become the lead climber, she should anchor on the side of the anchor and the belayer from which the next pitch will depart.

side of anchor that she intends to depart on the following lead. For example, if the pitch leads off to the right of the anchor, the second should anchor on the right side, so that once transition is complete, she can immediately lead in that direction. Swinging leads usually results in the quickest transitions, but it can be tiring because immediately after seconding a pitch, the second then becomes the leader. If the transition is swift, there is almost no rest for the second. By extension, the leader has to belay the second, then continue to sit, stand, or hang while belaying the new leader. That's a long time to spend at an anchor.

Blocking leads. The leader will lead again. When blocking leads, the second should anchor on the

The leader's side of the rope is stacked on the bottom.

A carefully stacked rope can be grabbed as one big pancake.

On block leads, the second restacks the rope while the leader re-racks. The belayer will want the leader's side of the rope to be on top of the stack.

opposite side of the leader's intended line of travel on the next pitch. For example, if the leader is belaying the second and intends to lead off to the left on the next pitch, he should anchor the belayer on the right. Blocking leads results in slightly slower transitions, but

If the second is about to lead, she sets up to the right.

If the second is about to belay, she sets up to the left.

LEAD

Leading in this direction

Means anchoring the second on this side.

If the leader is going to continue leading, the second should anchor on the opposite side of the leader's intended departure.

each climber gets a chance to rest before having to lead a pitch. On block leads, the belayer will also need to restack the rope so that the leader's end of the rope is on top of the stack.

Descents and Rappelling

O nce the climbing team arrives at the top of their climb, it's time to make a transition from going up to going down. For walk-offs, the transition is quick and easy. When the second arrives at the anchor, she can be given enough slack to walk toward the path or gully by which the team will descend. The second can be taken off belay once she has reached a safe distance from the cliff's edge, and then begin coiling the rope. The leader steps away from the cliff's edge, cleans the anchor,

Multistage rappels require a system that lets the rappel clip in to anchors with a tether and locking carabiner, but also extend the rappel. Double-length slings can easily do this, but the tether is short. It works great for steep rappels and hanging stations.

A cordelette can be rigged to extend a rappel and create a tether for anchor transitions.

Climbing manufacturers all produce PASes of various shapes and design. They all have unique features, and many climbers like to use these tools for multistage rappels.

and then joins her partner. The two can celebrate their ascent, change shoes, and begin their descent.

For rappels, the leader has to remember upon arriving at an anchor that the rappel will need to be rigged by passing the tail of rope through a rap

Once the second's rappel is set up and double-checked, the leader can take her off belay and set up her own rappel.

station. It's important for the leader to remember not to anchor the climbing rope with a clove hitch like he might normally do. Instead, the leader will want to construct a personal anchoring system using double-length slings, a cordelette, or a manufactured PAS. Now, while the leader belays the second, he can multi-task by setting up the rappel.

As the second arrives at an anchor, also preparing to make a transition from climbing to rappelling, there is no need to anchor with the climbing rope when he arrives. Since his partner has diligently prepared the rappel, he can construct a PAS of his own and immediately set up his rappel and auto-block backup. Once that system is assembled and double-checked, the second can be taken off belay. Now the leader can assemble his rappel directly in front to the second's rappel rig, on the uphill side. Once it's assembled and double-checked, the leader can clean the anchor, attach the rope ends to the second, and lower or saddlebag the climbing ropes for rappelling.

With both ends of the rope connected to the rappeller, there is no way to rappel off the ends of the rope.

Connecting the tails of rope to the first rappeller avoids the need to toss ropes, and it also helps the team avoid accidentally rappelling off the ends of the rope.

Carried on the brake hand side

Knotted rope ends

In windy conditions, or when there are lots of other climbers below, saddle bagging the ropes helps manage them during rappel.

Both rappellers are pre-rigged.

With the rappels pre-rigged, the climbers can quickly rappel to the next station and double check each other during the setup.

The rappelling sequence for most multipitch parties will unfold as described. The first rappeller has a friction-hitch backup and her rappel keeps the pre-rigged second rappeller backed up and stationary. As the first rappeller arrives at the next anchor, she will construct an anchor, attach herself to the masterpoint with her personal anchoring system, and finally unweight her rappel, providing enough slack for the second rappeller to begin moving. The first rappeller provides an attentive firefighter's belay to the second rappeller. Or if the party

An effective firefighter's belay is attentive, two hands ready to brake, arms outstretched and ready to pull down assertively.

A firefighter's belay is attentive, with two hands on the rope, ready to activate the rappeller's brake instantly.

If a rappeller loses control, firm downward pressure on both strands of rope will arrest the rappeller.

This firefighter's belay was activated just in time. Good thing the belayer was attentive!

so agrees, the second rappeller can tie her own friction-hitch backup so that the first rappeller can begin preparing the rappel station for transition.

As the second rappeller arrives at the anchor, either on firefighter's belay or her own backup, she uses her own personal anchoring system to connect to the masterpoint, alongside her partner. Both rappellers can now double-check their connections and disconnect from the rappel. Having arrived safely at this new

"OFF RAPPEL"

A full anchor and a single tether.

As each rappeller arrives at the anchor, she clips into the anchor with her tether. Both tethers should be double checked before the rappels and backups are deconstructed.

Room for the next rappeller to arrive.

The quad provides an attachment point for the second rappeller that is easy to recognize.

rappel station, they can begin the transition of the rope for the next rappel.

The transition from one rappel to the next is simple. The first rappeller can detach the tails of the

Simul-rappelling is a form of counterweight rappelling where two climbers use their own rappelling body mass to counterweight each other. It's an arrangement where two rappellers become completely interdependent, and therefore it has risks for an entire climbing team that are unique and severe. In a simul-rappelling arrangement, if one climber makes a mistake, a rigging error, inadequate backups, or severed rope; it endangers the counterweighted partner.

As a result, simul-rappelling is a technique that should only be selectively and carefully deployed. The risks it incurs are rarely justified by the teams that use the technique; it's deployed casually without acknowledgement or respect for how consequential small errors can be.

When the aggregated efficiencies of simul-rappelling have a measurable benefit, a team might consider learning to use the technique beforehand and then executing it safely and efficiently. For example, if a team has to execute lots of consecutive rappels, there can be measurable

rope from her harness, making sure all knots are clear from the tails of the rope. Then, she can pass one end of the rope through the rappel rings, connect that end of the rope to her harness, and continue threading the climbing rope through the rappel rings until reaching the middle. Meanwhile, the second rappeller can pull the rope down from the upper rappel station. Eventually the opposite end of the rope will fall down from the upper rappel station and tumble down the cliff. This opposite end of the rope should be retrieved and connected to the first rappeller; once again, she'll have

Both simul-rappellers are using ABDs.

Both simul-rappellers are tied to the end of their side of the rope.

Simul-rappelling makes the counterweighted rappellers vulnerable to each other's mistakes. It should only be used when the need for efficiency on consecutive rappels is imperative.

time benefits to simul-rappelling, if it's executed correctly. But that can be a shaky argument. After all, free soloing is faster than leading, anchoring, and belaying. Speed doesn't always justify severe risks.

both ends of the rope with her as she rigs the next rappel.

Finally, the team can begin the rappelling sequence anew. The first rappeller sets up her extended rappel and her backup. She watches as her partner sets up her own rappel on the uphill side. They double-check each other, and finally detach their personal anchors, clean their anchor, and begin the staged rappelling sequence anew. This process is repeated for each anchor down the entire descent.

CHAPTER 6

Anchoring

Multipitch climbing is one of the most imperative contexts for effective and creative anchor construction. On many climbs, just like in single-pitch sport and trad, the climbing team will discover well-placed modern bolts. Anchoring strategies from single pitch can easily be recycled for these common components. That's not to say that every bolt on every cliff doesn't deserve some healthy skepticism and a careful inspection, but generally the bolts on modern multipitch climbs will prove themselves trustworthy.

As a result, the rigging of these anchors will usually be quick and familiar. In multipitch climbing with bolted anchors, configurations like the quad provide

A quad anchor accommodates load directions that shift, and they have separate connection points for anchoring the leader, the second, and the belay.

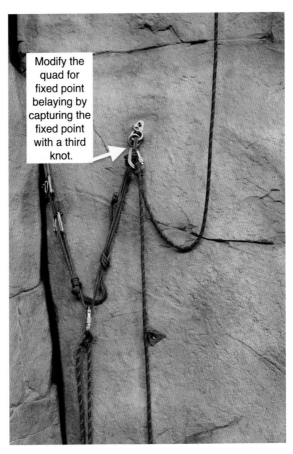

Modify the quad for fixed point belaying by capturing the fixed point with a third knot.

Cordelettes are long enough to rig a quad and a fixed point for direct belaying.

places to anchor the belay, belay the second, eventually anchor the second, and hang packs and accessories too. Furthermore, these configurations can be quickly modified to create a direct belay for a lead climber. They are amazingly versatile.

The tried-and-true ponytail anchor is still as strong, secure, and simple as ever.

Before self-adjusting anchoring systems like the quad became so popular, the basic ponytail anchor with cordelette or double-length sling was ubiquitous, and there is no good reason to distrust it. It still provides redundant rigging, a commodious masterpoint, and a shelf for attaching accessories.

Outside of these simple bolted anchors, multipitch climbing presents the kind of scenarios that both challenge the anchor builder to find effective solutions and unforgivingly punish her if she fails. Fall factors greater than 1, with adult body masses, can create the kinds of forces that could result in catastrophic anchor failure. The team has to get the anchoring right.

Why Do Anchors Fail?

Indisputably, anchors fail because the load the climbing team applies to the anchor exceeds the force that the anchor can withstand. Multipitch is one of the few contexts in climbing that can create loads of that magnitude. Given the manufactured strength of most removable protection gear, it is difficult to imagine a context where human body weights can create such loads. It's important to push the imagination on this point. What could make an anchor fail? There are few likely scenarios:

- Unperceived weaknesses in the anchor material, like UV deterioration, chemical contamination, or cuts and abrasions
- Weaker components, like components that are designed to hold less that 10kN of force
- Human error, like placing strong pieces poorly or placing them in poor rock

Those most likely errors give anchor builders some clear direction. It's important to select solid components, maintain reliable anchoring materials, and tie knots correctly.

Fundamental Principles of Anchoring

Since human error is the likely cause of most catastrophic anchor failures, it makes sense to think of fundamental anchoring principles that focus largely on averting that outcome. Many different acronyms have purported to do just that, but they're often confusing and misleading. By the time an anchor builder gets to multipitch, it's time for the anchor to achieve three unequivocal qualities, three simple ideas, all three equally valuable. If an anchor achieves these three essential qualities, it is most likely to avert human error.

Strength

An anchor must be strong enough to sustain all potential loads applied to it. Factor 2 falls, heavy climbers with packs full of gear, long falls, short falls: the anchor has to be strong enough to hold all of those loads. They are all potential loads.

Then, an anchor must be strong enough to pad the security of the system with a margin of error that could account for any number of mistakes that all humans are wont to make. Let's be conservative and provide ourselves with a 100 percent margin of error. That would mean that any anchor should be strong enough to sustain all potential loads applied to it, multiplied by two, for a 100 percent margin of error.

If we want to build anchors that can hold factor 2 falls and give the team a 100 percent margin of error, there have to be components in the system that can hold 10kN or more. Preferably, they can all hold 10kN or more. The strongest placements on most racks can

How strong is this anchor? It's hard to say. Hedge your bets. Imagine that it's only as strong as a single component, loaded one at a time.

For years, climbers have been instructed to calculate the strength of an anchor by adding up the sum of its parts. This tactic does not adhere to fundamental principles of physics, human factors of psychology, or a working understanding of rock quality and material science. The truth is that it is very difficult to predict how forces are being distributed to the components of an anchor. If that's true, then anchors don't really aggregate the load-bearing properties of their components. So the best guess as to the strength of an anchor points to the strength of a single component, until that component fails and the next component takes all the force.

hold 14kN, and so the strongest anchors have these kinds of components in them.

Security

We'll also roll up a bunch of historic ideas into one
central theme. Anchors should be secure. That means
that if anything unexpected happens—things break,
components fail, direction of load changes—the anchor
must survive those unexpected changes. Again, the
imagination is forced to conjure unlikely occurrences,
and those possibilities have to be compounded or

*Is this anchor secure? It looks like every point in the
rigging has backups.*

Is the anchor secure no matter which way you load it? Let's hope so. The security of an anchor should be unconditional.

discredited by probability. For example, we have data that demonstrates how rockfall can have traumatic effects on anchors, severing entire sections of an anchor. We have data that documents how sequential loads, shock loads, and loads in series affect an anchor. So we can know what kind of contingencies to prepare for and what kinds to generally ignore.

So an anchor that is secure has backups. It has systemic redundancy all the way to the masterpoint. If any single point in the anchor were to fail, other points provide adequate backups. We make a few exceptions for anchors that are so titanic in nature (large stable trees and boulders) that we might rely upon these single features alone, but even these features could be rigged in a redundant fashion.

Simplicity

Simplicity and efficiency are commonly combined ideas, and they are related. Basically, a climber needs to appreciate that any anchor can quickly become convoluted and overly complex if it is rigged to solve phantom hazards, unlikely/improbable contingencies, or adopt anchoring principles that are unachievable for reasons that are unsubstantiated.

For any given anchor, simplicity refers to the overall amount of time to construct and deconstruct an anchor. It should be minimized. Simplicity refers to the overall amount of equipment needed, including attachment materials, carabiners, components, and any amount of padding or edge protection as well. All that should be minimized. Simplicity also refers to the number of knots being tied and untied, the number of steps needed to construct the anchor, and the overall economy of movement required to build the anchor. All that should also be minimized too. When time, equipment, and number of steps are all minimized, and an anchor demonstrates adequate strength and security, an anchor will probably have achieved the best end result our current knowledge and technology can offer.

Anchor Complexity

There are three categorical circumstances that tend to make anchor building more complicated. These scenarios don't occur that often, so the techniques used to address them can usually be avoided outright with enough planning and forethought. Nevertheless, through one twist of fate or another, a climber will eventually encounter one of the following circumstances:

- The direction of load applied to an anchor will necessarily change. These scenarios usually involve lead climbing and directional placements. If a climber leads a pitch, the lead protection will create a direction of load that splits the vector between the fall line (where the belayer or counterweight load the anchor) and the last piece of protection (where the climber loads the anchor). Once those directionals are cleaned, both the climber and the belayer will load the anchor on the fall line. The direction of load changes significantly. Multipitch climbing can offer dramatic directional load changes too. Typically, the anchor is rigged to belay a second climber, and then the same anchor is used to anchor the lead belayer. The two loads could be completely different.

- Next, the components available for anchoring might be vastly dissimilar. On any given rack of traditional removable protection, for example, some cams are rated to hold over 14kNs, while the smallest cams may be rated to hold less than 6kNs. Asking these smaller pieces to do the same kind of load-bearing as their larger counterparts is not equitable; they are not equally valuable components. When anchoring components have vastly dissimilar load-bearing properties, the rigging will have to be more complicated.

- Lastly, a climber often has to construct an anchor with limited resources. When resources are scant, the values and principles of anchoring do not change. But building a fundamentally sound anchor with limited resources is very challenging. It often requires some innovative and artistic problem-solving, hence the complexity.

Hopefully the reader will notice my aversion to using the word "equalization" to describe how load is distributed to the components in an anchor. The resilience of this word and this idea sits in defiance of everything that we know about anchors. Anchors never really distribute equal load to the components, and even if they did, we wouldn't have any way to verify that it is happening. Yet, people continue to use this word. Climbing instructors and guides continue to teach people to think of anchors in this way. I hope you'll try to eliminate this word and this idea from your anchoring lexicon. Even the conceptual notion of a perfect load distribution will only distract you from the concepts that really matter in anchor building: Select *strong* components. Think of the overall *security* of the anchor when you rig the masterpoint. And try to keep it all as *simple* as possible. —RF

Learning Anchor Craft

Traditional multipitch climbing demands the anchor builder be creative, thoughtful, and skilled. There is no such thing as a multipitch climb where anchoring skills are not an integral and unavoidable part of the security of the team. So a climber that may not have learned to anchor through single-pitch climbing might legitimately ask: If I need to anchor well to multipitch climb, how do I learn?

Step 1: Study

Take some time to read books and articles about anchoring. Read the research those books and articles are based on. All the information that anyone needs to know about anchoring is available in scores. Appreciate that anchoring is an art and a craft, and all great artists and craftspeople study their craft.

Step 2: Become an Anchor Analyst

Climbers can have relationships to the craft of anchoring long before they start actually constructing their own anchors. Climbing with a skilled anchor builder can provide dozens of working examples of the craft. But there is a big difference between a passive relationship to someone else's handiwork, cleaning and using the anchors without consideration or analysis, and using every anchor encountered to dissect the skills and decision-making that were used to create them.

For every anchor, ask the following questions:

1. Is the anchor fundamentally sound? Is it strong, secure, and simple?

2. If not, why? Are the components and attachments weak? Could a single incident result in a catastrophic failure? Was the anchor unnecessarily complex and time-consuming?

3. Was the anchor builder managing one of the circumstances that necessarily complicates anchor building? Is the solution also fundamentally sound?

When you analyze anchors, try to appreciate that alternatives abound. There are dozens of ways to build fundamentally sound anchors. At first, it's difficult to tell the difference between an option and a principled optimization. Typically, if an anchor is overbuilt, it is not as simple as it could be. The simpler option optimizes the fundamental principles.

Step 3: Ground School

Head out to a boulder field or the base of a crag, and build anchors. Analyze the anchors you build. It's easy nowadays to take a photo of your anchor, send it to a friend or an instructor, and ask for feedback. It's better to make these experiments (and mistakes) in a risk-neutral setting.

Step 4: Take a Class or Hire a Guide

Formal instruction from a good climbing instructor or a guide with a knack for teaching can be the most efficient way to know what you don't know. A professional can see the patterns in your skill set that you can't see because you are still learning.

Step 5: Ease into Real Anchoring on Real Climbs

Some climbs present nightmare scenarios for a climber in a formative phase of their anchor building. A climb like Culp-Bossier on Hallett's Peak in Rocky Mountain National Park, for example, might present some attractively moderate climbing, but the anchoring situations can be terribly complicated. The rock can be poor, the leads can exhaust the rack, and the directionality of the anchor can be widely variable. It's a 5.8 climb, but it's got 5.14 anchoring challenges all over it.

Instead, select climbs that have straightforward anchoring challenges and moderate climbing difficulties. Look for lines that climb a continuous crack system. Odds are, the anchoring will consistently be in that system. Avoid climbs that have traverses, roofs, or downclimbs off the belay. These climbs will all require anchors that adjust to wildly variable load directions.

Dealing with Problems

There are so many potential problems in multi-pitch climbing, they boggle the mind. An entire book could be dedicated to the techniques needed to execute and intervene. The scope of this tiny book cannot answer all the questions or show all the techniques. Reluctantly, we'll focus on four scenarios that are likely to happen to every multipitch climber eventually.

Scenario 1. It's easy to imagine that you'll eventually take a lead fall, or your partner will take a fall, and you'll get hurt. Most of the time, these injuries are minor, but they often put an end to the climbing for the day. You're going to need to bail.

Scenario 2. It is highly likely that the seconding climber will fall on some climb or another. Most of the time, grateful for the attentive belay, they get back on the climb and keep climbing. But eventually, the multipitch team will encounter a scenario where the seconding climber cannot get back on the moves. Maybe she's dangling from an overhang and can no longer reach the rock. Maybe she's fallen down to a section of climbing without holds or footing. Either way, she's going to need some help.

Scenario 3. Eventually you're going to pull your rappel rope and it's going to get stuck. You're going to need that rope for the rest of your rappels. You have to go get it.

Scenario 4. Eventually, you're going to drop or forget a belay rappel device. You'll need to know how to improvise one.

Bailing and Tandem Rappelling

Scenario 1. There are so many ways that the leader rescue scenario can inextricably encumber a climbing team: the leader can't be lowered back to the belay, being more than half the rope length up a long pitch, dangling off an overhang, or having traversed onto a fall line that will not reach the original belay. It's a complicated situation. In this case we'll focus on an easy version that is more common.

The leader has taken a lead fall, twisted an ankle, and is now suspended 30 feet above the belay. The team is on the third pitch of a five-pitch climb. The belayer lowers the leader back down to the belay and anchors the leader with a personal anchor that is

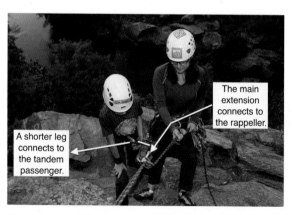

Tandem rappelling lets one person get a ride from his partner. It's a great skill to know if one climber is injured.

separate from the climbing rope. Once the leader is anchored, the second can begin packaging and stabilizing the leader's ankle.

From this point, the belayer will do most of the rigging, leaving the leader to tend to his ankle.

The belayer takes all the equipment and rigs for tandem rappel. He'll rappel with his climbing partner guarding his wounded ankle.

Lowers, Raises, and Rope Ascension

Scenario 2. In the second scenario there are few options, and they each involve a unique technical skill set: The second has fallen and cannot regain climbing holds. The belayer could lower the second down to access features that can be climbed. The belayer could create a hauling system to pull the climber up to features that can be climbed. Or the climber could ascend the belay rope.

Before attempting to open the plaquette, the friction hitch backup is in place and the brake strand has been redirected.

Lowering. The loaded auto-blocking tool is difficult to manage as manufacturers recommend. Instead, the belayer applies a friction hitch backup, redirects the brake strand, and then opens the plaquette. For

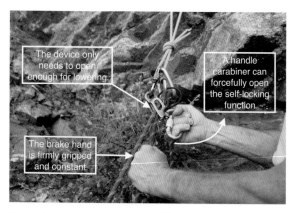

A carabiner in the nose ring of the plaquette can be used to pry open the plaquette with one hand while the other hand maintains the brake.

For longer lowers, the blocking carabiner can be levered back toward the anchor with a sling and the belayer's body weight.

short lowers, a carabiner can wrench the plaquette open. For longer lowers, a sling can be used to pull the blocking carabiner out of the plaquette position.

Hauling. A simple mechanical advantage can be created by tying a friction hitch to the loaded strand, a carabiner can be connected to that, and the brake strand can be clipped into that. The resulting three-to-one mechanical advantage is diminished by significant friction from the plaquette and the carabiners. But with some effort, it can be used to raise the climb a short distance.

Friction hitch

3:1 Hauling won't work for everyone, but for many it provides just enough mechanical advantage to give the second climber assistance from above.

Climbing the rope. In many versions of this scenario, the belayer cannot see or communicate with the climber. The climber might shout and shout for assistance but never receive it. The climber is on his own; he's forced to climb back up to holds and footing on the climbing rope. In this sequence a friction hitch and double-length sling can be connected to the climbing rope. This stirrup, or improvised platform, will let the climber stand up and in the process introduce enough slack to insert an assisted braking device. Now, the assisted braking device can capture progress as the climber ascends.

Ascending a Rope and Protecting the Ascent

Scenario 3: When pulling a rappel rope from above, the climbing team actually makes a very risky gamble every time. The chore is just so common, it's easy to overlook how fraught it actually is. To put it another way, the climbing team is willing to allow 30m of climbing rope (sometimes up to 60m when two ropes are conjoined by a bulky joining knot) tumble through terrain with cracks, protrusions, horns, flakes, loose rock, vegetation, and other people nearby, and every time there is an expectation that over 100 feet of randomly swirling and lassoing rope will not get

A friction hitch and a foot loop

From the dangling position, the climber can tie a friction hitch and foot loop to the climbing rope.

Standing up on the footloop generates some slack.

Standing on that loop generates slack. The climber could even connect his belay loop to the friction hitch here to maintain his position.

Apply an ABD to the slack

He can now rig his progress-capture. An ABD like a GriGri works great.

Ascension system:
-Ascender
-Footloop
-Progress-capture (ABD)

All the elements of rope ascension are in place: an ascender, a progress-capture, and a definitive connection to the rope.

snagged on any of the potential booby traps anywhere along that fall line.

Frankly, it's surprising the rope doesn't get stuck every time.

Eventually every team will get the rope stuck, and when they do there are three possible scenarios. In the first—the easiest—the climbing team still has access to both ends of the climbing rope. In this scenario the team can ascend both strands of rope up to where the

Build an ascension system that climbs both ropes.

This ascension system climbs two ropes instead of one using an ATC Guide.

problem is, solve the problem, ensure the snag does not happen again, and then continue rappelling.

In the second scenario the rope is still running through the rappel station above, but the one tail of the rope is snagged along the climb somewhere.

While climbing the jammed rope, tie in to the other end of the rope, take a belay, and protect the pitch as you ascend.

Climbing this rope with no backup is sketchy. Take a belay on the opposite end of the rope, and protect the pitch as you ascend.

The climber can ascend the stuck rope, but it's hard to know how secure the snag is. What if it pops out while the climber is ascending the rope? As a result, the climber will also need to tie in to the opposite end of the rope, take a rack and belay, and protect the pitch as she ascends the jammed rope. In this manner if the rope dislodges during her ascent, she will take a lead fall, but her belayer will have an opportunity to catch her.

Once she arrives at the snag, she can attach herself to both sides of the rappel rope with a friction hitch, or she can attach herself to an anchor that she constructs. Either way, she'll need to unsnag the opposite tail, conjoin the two tails, and transition to rappelling.

In the third version of this problem, the rope has pulled all the way through the upper rap station and the tail has snagged along the fall line. Again, the climber can ascend the snagged rope, but it's hard to know how secure the snag is. What if it pops out while the climber is ascending the rope? As a result, the climber will also need to tie in to the opposite end of the rope, take a rack and belay, and protect the pitch as she ascends the jammed rope. In this manner if the rope dislodges during her ascent, she will take a lead fall, but her belayer will have an opportunity to catch her.

This time, when the climber arrives at the snag, the rope is no longer connected to an upper rap station above. The climber will have to construct an anchor that she intends to abandon and use that anchor as the point from which to unsnag her rope and resume rappelling.

Scenario 4. Eventually, you're going to drop or forget a belay rappel device. You'll need to know

The carabiner brake provides enough friction for smooth rappelling.

how to improvise one. Improvised rappels and belays are very useful once they're understood and available. Many parties use these techniques routinely once they get the hang of them. There is an elegance to doing more with less equipment.

To build the one-way munter:

1) Pull the brake strand and shift the munter into the take position.

2) Clip the biting loop of the hitch to the load strand.

The one-way Munter feels like an auto-blocking belay tool. It will allow the multipitch belayer to multitask.

For rappelling, one of the most common versions is the carabiner brake. It works just like any belay device, and it only requires four nonlocking carabiners to assemble.

For belaying, the Munter hitch will work for any direct belay; it will work for belaying the leader or belaying the second. When belaying the second, it's difficult to multitask with a Munter in the same way that one does with an auto-blocking belay tool. So a simple gesture can turn a Munter hitch into something that feels and belays like a plaquette. The one-way Munter is constructed by pulling the Munter into a "take" position and then connecting the biting loop of the hitch back to the load strand with a locking carabiner.

CHAPTER 8

Practicing Multipitch Skills

As one can imagine, practicing the multiple steps and little sequences of multipitch takes practice. Actual multipitch climbs are some of the worst places to practice. The team is exposed, the time-consuming errors are conspicuous, and the learning team is usually monopolizing a real rock climb for lessons that could happen more effectively (and more safely) in ground school.

Guides and Expert Mentors

It's nice to start one's multipitch career by seeing it perfectly executed. Hiring a certified guide to show you multipitch efficiency and precise rope work and to point out all the little details is a valuable use of time. Taking a class is a similarly valuable exercise.

If you are hiring a guide, make sure to remember the point of the exercise: You want to see perfectly executed multipitch. So be sure to hire a well-trained and credentialed guide. Be sure that she is going to guide you on a route that she knows really well, one that she can execute perfectly. Even guides make mistakes, and they usually correct their errors quickly, but you don't want to see errors. You are paying for perfection.

You should have the same expectations of an expert mentor, but it's harder (and rude) to be so directive to someone that is volunteering their time. You might have to cajole a mentor with flattery and beer.

Multipitch Ground School

Eventually, you'll need to go to a public park or forest, preferably on a wooded hillside, and experiment with your partner. Belay your partner up and practice communication. Practice transitions and belaying the second. Improvise some rappel anchors and practice a multistaged descent. If you make a mistake in ground school, you might be a little embarrassed, and at worst you might even tumble into some grass or leaves. The same mistake on an actual rock climb will be much more costly. After the hillside you might graduate to a 4th-Class gully. You can actually build anchors and place lead protection in a gully or ravine. Be careful of loose rock in these features.

Single-Pitch Prep

As previously mentioned, single-pitch crags are great places to train for multipitch. A single-pitch crag is a great place to experiment with unfamiliar movement styles and new rock types. It's also a great place to experiment with hanging belays.

You can practice belaying a second by belaying at the top of a climb and then making a transition on to rappel, just like you would do at the top of a multipitch climb. This is not only good practice, it's actually a more efficient way to single-pitch. The hanging belays can get uncomfortable, but the practice is just what you need. Practice rope

Next time you're at a single-pitch crag, rig up a hanging belay and practice belaying a leader and catching falls. The jarring sensation will take some getting used to.

Even if everyone might think it's weird, belaying at the top of a single-pitch crag is great training for multipitch climbing.

management, practice belaying the second. Practice hauling up a pack.

Single-pitch trad venues with walk-off descents are also great places to go mini-multipitch climbing. A 40-foot section of rope will turn a 100-foot single

Better to learn off-width technique here than a thousand feet off the ground.

pitch into a three-pitch climb. These are types of experiments to make after lots of ground school, and hopefully not on really popular climbs, but the mileage is invaluable.

Those mini-multipitch climbs are also great places to practice improvised rescue scenarios.

Boulder Field Prep

Boulder fields are great places to experiment with new movement styles and new rock types as well. They're also great places to practice building anchors. You can explore the cracks and pockets to hone your skills with anchor building.

Horizons

There is so much more to multipitch than this text can cover. The contents are hopefully designed to make climbers thoughtful in their planning and preparation, selective of their partners and objectives, and minimally skilled to begin learning to multipitch. After the contents of this book are understood, rehearsed, and deployed a few times, the horizons and multitudinous questions will begin to emerge.

Here are a few of the things that we did not cover in great depth in this book, but you will eventually want to learn more about.

More-Advanced Multipitch Climbing

Different forms of multipitch climbing, forms that are outside of our definition, will eventually attract attention. For each of these forms, there are vast and new skills that cannot be intuited from the contents of this book. They will require the same care and intention to learn as learning to multipitch rock climb.

Alpine rock climbing. Adding mixed precipitation, bivouac, altitude, and new climbing equipment to the rock-climbing repertoire (crampons, axes, snow protection) means that climbing teams can explore the mountains, where the new array of objective and environmental hazards present a new array of adventures.

Snow, altitude, and bivouac make alpine rock climbing a more complex pursuit.

Big-wall climbing. Scaling rock climbs that drift into Grade V, VI, and VII require enormous work, commitment, and careful planning. Usually, on multi-pitch climbs of this scale, so much extra equipment is needed that every pitch is punctuated by the management and hauling of that equipment. On sheer walls where natural ledges are unavailable, climbers deploy

The big stone is ominous and alluring. It takes dedication and new skills to climb big walls.

portable collapsible ledges, from which they can belay, relax, or bivy. Aid climbing and climbing fixed ropes are both technical components of big-wall climbing that are fun and engaging, but they also take practice and a unique skill set.

New Technical Skills

A variety of technical skills that are not covered in this book will eventually emerge and suggest themselves. They all have merit in some way or another.

Leading with double ropes. Leading and being belayed by two ropes offers many advantages on terrain where protection is not available along a single fall line. The technique takes skill and practice for both a belayer and a leader to manage.

Moving as a rope team. Shortening the rope between two climbers and moving continuously over easy 5th-Class terrain, or more commonly 3rd- and 4th-Class terrain, is a skill that many rock climbers eventually learn to get down complex descents that aren't quite severe enough to rappel, nor secure enough to simply hike.

Simul-climbing and speed climbing. The techniques involved in simul-climbing, where both climbers ascend 5th-Class terrain simultaneously using the intermittent protection of the rope to protect them both, exposes both climbers to each other's falls, to the hazards between the two climbers, and to opportunities for long falls. Simul-climbing is fast though. Without intermediate anchors and belays or any associated problems, snags, or falls, the climbing team can flow right up the cliff.

These climbers have shortened the amount of rope between them. That way they can give each other backup when they need it.

Lots of Improvised Rescue Scenarios to Practice

Improvised rescue or small-teams rescue requires vastly variable problem-solving. Our text does not cover increasing mechanical advantage in raising systems, a dozen forms of load transfer to get a stranded or incapacitated climber from one connection to the next. We did not cover transitions to counterbalance lowers or rappels, and we avoided complex leader rescue in particular. These skills are fun to learn, and a competent mentor, instructor, or guide can teach them.

Different Climbing Teams

Conspicuously, this book did not cover climbing teams of three. For some objectives, finding the right person to pair with is challenging. Finding two is even more challenging. Too often, when multipitch climbing teams form groups of three of four, someone in the team is not yet skilled enough to participate in multipitch climbing without mentorship. As previously mentioned, the moral responsibility of mentoring others is severe. Professional guides train to take that responsibility, and informal mentors should take the responsibility equally seriously.

If the team members are appropriately skilled though, a team of three can move quite efficiently in multipitch. But they'll need to learn to manage a more complex rope system. They'll need to learn when and how to belay two people simultaneously or belay each other one at time. A party of three climbing is so vastly different than a party of two, in terms of rope

Introducing another rope and another climber doubles the complexity of the rope work and the decision-making.

work and decision-making, it is discouraged for all but the most skilled practitioners.